THE ORESTEIA

AESCHYLUS

THE

ORESTEIA

A NEW TRANSLATION BY

TED HUGHES

FARRAR, STRAUS AND GIROUX

NEW YORK

Farrar, Straus and Giroux
18 West 18th Street, New York 10011

Copyright © 1999 by The Estate of Ted Hughes
Printed in the United States of America
Originally published in 1999 by Faber and Faber Ltd, Great Britain
Published in the United States in 1999
by Farrar, Straus and Giroux
First Farrar, Straus and Giroux paperback edition, 2000

This version of THE ORESTEIA
was commissioned by the Royal National Theatre
for performance in the fall of 1999.

Library of Congress Control Number: 98-073704

ISBN-13: 978-0-374-52705-1
ISBN-10: 0-374-52705-9

www.fsgbooks.com

14   16   17   15

Contents

AGAMEMNON

DRAMATIS PERSONAE

AGAMEMNON

King of Argos, son of Atreus, and victor at Troy

CLYTEMNESTRA

Queen of Argos, daughter of Leda

AEGISTHUS

Thyestes' son, Atreus' nephew, and Clytemnestra's lover

CASSANDRA

*daughter of Priam, King of Troy; a prophetess,
and slave to Agamemnon*

WATCHMAN

citizen of Argos

HERALD

Greek soldier come from Troy

CHORUS

Elders of Argos

Guards of Aegisthus

(Outside the royal palace at Argos.)

WATCHMAN

You Gods in heaven—
You have watched me here on this tower
All night, every night for twelve months,
Thirteen moons—
Tethered on the roof of this palace
Like a dog.
It is time to release me.
I've stared long enough into this darkness
For what never emerges.
I'm tired of the constellations—
That glittering parade of lofty rulers
Night after night a little bit earlier
Withholding the thing I wait for—
Slow as torture.
And the moon, coming and going—
Wearisome, like watching the sea
From a deathbed. Like watching the tide
In its prison yard, with its two turns
In out in out.
I'm sick of the heavens, sick of the darkness.
The one light I wait for never comes.
Maybe it never will come—
A beacon-flare that leaps from peak to peak
Bringing the news from Troy—
'Victory! After ten years, Victory!'
The one word that Clytemnestra prays for.
Queen Clytemnestra—who wears
A man's heart in a woman's body,
A man's dreadful will in the scabbard of her body
Like a polished blade. A hidden blade.
Clytemnestra reigns over fear.
I get up sodden with dew.
I walk about, to shift my aches.
I lie down—the aches harden worse.
No dreams. No sleep. Only fear—

Fear like a solid lump of indigestion
Here, high in my belly—a seething.
Singing's good for fear
But when I try to sing—weeping comes.
I weep. There's no keeping it down.
Everything's changed in this palace.
The old days,
The rightful King, order, safety, splendour,
A splendour that lifted the heart—
All gone.
You Gods,
Release me.
Let that flame come leaping out of the East
To release me.
Where did that light come from? In pitch darkness
That point—that's new.
Down there, near what must be the skyline,
In the right place! It just appeared!
A flickering point. And getting bigger. A fire!
The beacon!
Tell the Queen—
It's the beacon.
It's flaring up! It's shaking its horns.
Troy has fallen.
The King is coming home.
Agamemnon is coming. Troy has fallen!
Now the Queen can rejoice
And I'll be the first to dance—Troy has fallen.
The gods have blessed our master.
They've blessed me too.
They've made me the bearer of the news.
Only let them bring the King home safely.
Let me prostrate myself at his feet
And then—what follows,
Better not think about it.
Only the foundations of this house
Can tell that story. Yes,
The tongue that could find

The words for what follows—that tongue
Would have to lift this house's foundations.
Those who know too much, as I do, about this house,
Let their tongue lie still—squashed flat.
Under the foundations.

(Cry of triumph from Clytemnestra inside palace. She enters: casts incense on altars, etc. Enter Elders of Argos: the Chorus. Dawn.)

CHORUS

Ten years ago
The sons of Atreus,
Menelaus and Agamemnon,
Both divine Kings,
Assembled a thousand ships
Crammed with the youth of Hellas
And sailed across the sea to punish Priam.

Two brothers, ravenous for war,
Their hunger for war
Went up
Like the screaming
Of eagles, two eagles in agony
Over a crag
Where their nest has been robbed—
Beating the air
With broad oars,
Climbing the currents
They bewail, in helpless fury,
Their lost labours.
Their brood gone,
They lament
Their vigilance that failed.
Anguish tears their throats.
They scream it in heaven—and in heaven
Some god hears it—
Zeus or Pan

Or Apollo hears
And pities it,
And sends a remorseless fury
To hunt the culprit down
And pluck the guilt from his bowels.

So now Zeus—protector
Of the sacred trust
Between the guest and the host—
Sends the two sons of Atreus
To rip the boasting tongue
From between the lips of Paris
And Helen from his bed.
Greece and Troy with bellowing effort
Lock their limbs
In that accursed marriage, and labour
At the killing.
Spear-shafts splinter
In twisting bodies,
Strong men kneel
In their own blood
Under weights of darkness
And what is happening
Cannot be otherwise.
Cannot not happen.
Fate holds every man
Of these two embattled armies
By the scruff of the neck
And jams his face, helpless,
Into what has to happen.
Priam pours libations
To lubricate the favour of the heavens
In vain.
He burns perfumed offerings on altars
To soften their pity
In vain.
The gods above and the gods below
Ignore him.

No bribes,
Nothing that passes under the roof of a temple
Or under the roof of the mouth,
Can appease heaven's anger
Or deflect its aim.
We were too old.
Second childhood
Propped on sticks
Kept us out of the battle.
We stayed here
On the scrap heap
Playing with our dreams,
The playthings of dreams.

(Chorus sees Clytemnestra.)

Queen Clytemnestra,
What has happened?
What have you heard?
Why have you called for a sacrifice
Throughout Argos—
Every altar
Of every god
Is ablaze—
From the kitchen-shrines of hearth-goblins
To the high temple of Zeus, god of the summits.
Fortunes in rich oil
Go up in smoke
Smudging the dawn.
Cherished beasts
Drop to their knees
In a flood of blood.
What has happened?
What is happening?
Are we right
To smell hope
In all this?
Or has a worse fear come? Tell us.

Do all these fiery tongues,
These forked and horned offerings,
Declare good news or the opposite? Tell us.
Do they consume the evil of the past
And the dread of what is to come—
All these fears that sicken us—
Or do they thicken the air with something worse?

I am the man to tell this tale.
Old age
Takes away everything
Except a few words the gods have tested,
For the eye
That opens towards the grave
Sees the core of things and is prophetic.
As our two Kings set out,
As their floating forest of spears
Lifted anchor,
Two birds,
Hook-beaked, big-winged birds,
A black bird and a white bird,
Sailed over
On the right—on the right!
Good fortune!
The whole army cheered the good omen—
Victory!

Then those two birds,
The black bird and the white bird,
Flushed and drove and killed
A hare heavy with her twins.
The whole army
Saw them kill the pregnant hare. They saw
The black bird and the white bird
That had brought them promise of victory
Rip the mother's womb and drag from it
The living unborn tenants—
The whole army watched from start to finish

That murder of the unborn.
If evil is in this wind, let it blow over.

Calchas the seer
Recognised the birds,
The white bird and the black,
Menelaus and Agamemnon.
Calchas
Cried to the whole army and the two Kings:
'What does this kill mean? I will tell you.
It means
Victory with a twist.
Fate will destroy
All Troy's cattle,
All Troy's crops,
And at last
Will open to you the city's holy of holies.
But when you have emptied Troy of her blood and her
    babies,
Then you can expect the anger of heaven.
Artemis, the moon-faced, the goddess,
The mother of the hares,
Beautiful Artemis,
Deity of the womb and its mystery,
Protectress of mothers and their darlings,
She has heard the death-cry of the hare,
She has seen what her father's birds have done,
She has looked through the bloody spy-hole
Where the hare's womb was plucked out.
She has seen the bigger murder behind it
Still to be committed
By the hooked heads,
The white bird and the black bird—
What will she do now?
Will she bless the triumph of the great birds—
Will she forgive
The ripping out of the womb? Can she forgive
The death-cry, inaudible to man,

Of the unborn?
Apollo, healing god,
Apollo,
Heal the wound in the bowels of your sister,
Allay her anger, quiet her frenzy
Before she exacts a compensation
That none of us can pay,
Before she pins the fleet in the lee of some island
Under a fixed wrong wind,
Forcing the two Kings
To sacrifice
A thing they hardly dare look at,
A beloved, bewildered, lovely creature,
A sacrifice that cannot be eaten,
A sacrifice that poisons the heart
And pours its blood into this palace,
Filling the furious womb of the woman
Who waits in this palace—
Avenging Artemis, who stands
Casting the shadow of a great Queen.
Then Clytemnestra's shadow
Takes the shape of a sprawling murdered man.
And the bloody footprints of Clytemnestra
Become those of a sacrificed child—
Bloody footprints staggering through this palace
Generation to generation.'

This is how Calchas the seer
Unriddled the murder of the hare.
With a foregone, god-given victory
He opened the ear of Agamemnon
To the first whisper of a curse
And opened his heart to the fatal
Contradiction of heaven.

But then he soothed him with hope—
A hope of ultimate good.
What is good? Who is God? The mask

Of the great nameless.
Who can say anything about it?
I call God Zeus
And Zeus, or the greater one
Who wears Zeus like a mask for man to imagine,
Has given man this law:
The truth
Has to be melted out of our stubborn lives
By suffering.
Nothing speaks the truth,
Nothing tells us how things really are,
Nothing forces us to know
What we do not want to know
Except pain.
And this is how the gods declare their love.
Truth comes with pain.

Agamemnon
Heard the terror stirring and looming
Through the words of the seer.
But he was no longer a man in a man's body
Confronting the lonely fate
That would kill him.
He was a war-machine,
A launched campaign, a whole nation of vengeance.
His profile was the prow of a thousand ships.
Meanwhile, the wrong wind had caught our fleet
And pinned us under the lee of Aulis.
Everything followed.
A big sea built off the point.
It was the wall of a prison. In that bay
The whole army lay trapped. The weeks passed.
The rigging of the ships rotted.
And the men fermented. In the squalls
Ships dragged their anchors, gored each other,
Crushed each other's ribs, wrecked each other,
Then broke up in the surf, against rocks.
Stores dwindled and mouldered.

Men's minds started to go.
Explosions of boredom, screaming quarrels.
Senseless killings. Mutinies, desertions,
Feuds between factions. Finally, the sickness.
Under that locked wind
The overcrowded prison that had been an army
Became a hospital.

At that point Calchas the seer
Spoke for heaven. He told us
What had to be done
To shift that wind—
When they heard what Artemis demanded
The warlords cried out,
Incredulous.
But Agamemnon—Agamemnon
When he heard it
Roared with anguish
Sudden as the wound of a night-arrow.
They took it in, those chieftains,
With a jabbering of grief.
Their royal staves
Pounded the earth.
Then Agamemnon, our general for good reason,
Mastered himself, with painful words:
If I obey the goddess, my own daughter
Has to die.
If I deny the goddess, this whole army
Has to dissolve.

If I obey the goddess, and kill my daughter—
What do I become?
A monster to myself, to the whole world,
And to all future time, a monster—
Wearing my daughter's bloody dress
Like a turban. The King of cruelty.
Painting my royal palace afresh
With her blood, the blood of Iphigenia.

Perfuming my bath, after the battle,
With the blood of Iphigenia.
Filling the drinking cups of my family
With the blood of Iphigenia—
This is how I shall live on in men's minds.

But if I deny the goddess, then what happens?
Will it be worse?
An utter defeat
For us all. And for me—
Disaster. As if I deserted this army,
Disguised, a traitor to my oath,
Shorn of honour,
Shunning men, shunned by men,
And wherever men gossip together
A term of contempt. An outcast on the earth.
The rest of my life skulking in corners,
Afraid of my own name.

If my daughter dies—the winds change,
Artemis is happy.
Our allied armies revive, as at a word
The sail fills with a breath.
And I have done no more
Than sacrifice myself—myself,
Not only my daughter but also my daughter's father.
So ought every warrior to live—
As if already dead.

With these words, Agamemnon surrendered
To necessity. As if snatched up
Into the chariot
Of his own madness.
And inside himself, secretly,
With a roar like rage, to deafen himself,
He murders his own daughter, Iphigenia.
Then orders the public sacrifice
Of this girl whose blood

Already streams through his future.
The decision, fixed in a moment,
Drags him,
As at the heels of horses,
Into that future
Where the blood of his daughter
Collects and waits for him
In a pool—

So the great King, Agamemnon,
Launches his thousand keels
On the blood of a virgin.
To reclaim a stolen whore.
Iphigenia for Helen.
He takes what he wants—and he pays for it.

When Agamemnon spoke,
Those chieftains, in the blink of an eye,
Became every man an Agamemnon—
Famished for the war.
A gale of war roars through them
Like a gale of visions—the battle-fury,
The massacres to come, and the glory
Lift Iphigenia's virgin life,
A straw in a great wind—

The prayers go up. Her father
Gives the signal. Iphigenia
Is hoisted off her feet by attendants—
They hold her over the improvised altar
Like a struggling calf.
The wind presses her long dress to her body
And flutters the skirt, and tugs at her tangled hair—
'Daddy!' she screams. 'Daddy!'—
Her voice is snatched away by the boom of the surf.
Her father turns aside, with a word
She cannot hear. She chokes—
Hands are cramming a gag into her mouth.

They bind it there with cord, like a horse's bit.
Her lovely lips writhe at the curb.
So the cry that by chance
Might have cursed the house of Atreus
Is trapped inside her body,
Heaving her breasts.
Now rough hands rip off her silks
And the wind waltzes with them
Down across the beach, and over the surf.
Her eyes swivel in their tears.
She recognises her killers—
Men who had wept
To hear her sing in the home of Agamemnon
When wine was poured out for the high gods.
They clench their hearts hard
And avoid her eyes.
They stare at a masterpiece of perfect skin
Goose-pimpled in the cold.
Pity is like a butterfly in a fist
As the knuckles whiten.

I saw nothing else—I could not watch it.
But I shall see
The words of the prophet fulfilled—
Every act
Rouses, like a sleeping law, in the atom,
What will balance it.
Then the truth
Comes as a shock of unexpected pain.
If it must come, when it comes
There'll be time to bewail it.

Who knows what will be?
The final balance of the truth,
The truth in its orbit of repose,
Has to be good.
Let it be good. Only let it be good.
This is the prayer

Of old men
Left to defend the empty throne of Argos
While Agamemnon, our King,
Still at sea, in the hour before dawn,
Gropes home through the labyrinth of his fate.

(Clytemnestra confronts the Elders.)

Clytemnestra, we honour you,
In the absence of Agamemnon.
The King gone, we honour his Queen.
What is the news?
Good or bad?
That kindles the fires
On all these altars.
Or is it only a rumour? One more rumour?
We hardly dare ask, but our loyalty
Makes us bold.

CLYTEMNESTRA
Good news should be delivered in a glory
Like the sun itself, from the womb of night.
This dawn is like a daughter to me—
More beautiful than hope dared to imagine.
Troy has fallen, and our Kings have sacked it.

CHORUS
Troy has fallen? That is impossible.

CLYTEMNESTRA
Troy has fallen. My words say what I mean.

CHORUS
What am I to do? I am weeping.

CLYTEMNESTRA
Those tears are the tears of loyal men.

CHORUS

Who can be certain? How can Troy have fallen?

CLYTEMNESTRA

Only a lying god could have deceived me.

CHORUS

Maybe while you slept, a dream deceived you.

CLYTEMNESTRA

Do you think I am one to be swayed by a dream?

CHORUS

Maybe a rumour. We embrace what's welcome.

CLYTEMNESTRA

You think me a feeble girl? Do you know who I am?

CHORUS

When did Troy fall?

CLYTEMNESTRA

Last night, last night!
This glorious morning is born out of it—
This huge blaze out of the East.

CHORUS

How could news get here? So far? So fast?

CLYTEMNESTRA

A god of fire sprang from the peak of Ida
And swift as a glance with news of the fall of Troy
Alit in flames on Hermes' crag—
The tip-top height of Lemnos. Leapt again
And landed on Athos. There in a flash,
The rock of Zeus was ablaze—
And my watchers were ready to feed it.
Then that flame took off, in a frenzy,

With a single stride it crossed the Aegean —
One giant wingbeat of lightning,
Showering the sea with glitter,
Bringing fish up out of the depths to be dazzled —
It landed on the heights of Makistos.
The watchman there was awake, he refreshed it
With a gloomy stack of timber,
And flung its fiery word, like a meteor,
Over the dark lands
To the channel of Euripus,
Where the Messapian guards were waiting for it.
They fed it with heath and thorns.
Stronger than ever, in a single bound
It crossed the plain of Asopus
And landed like the glare of the moon
On the crags of Cithaeron. The watchman there
Urged it on, with a crackling explosion,
From a tower of conifer trunks.
It soared over the swamp of Gorgopis
To the mountaineers awake in Aegiplanctus —
Overjoyed they heaped their beacon
With everything that would burn.
Then the far-travelled flame, redoubled,
Shook its tongues and leapt
Across the headland by the gulf of Saronis,
Touched the crag of Arachne
That overlooks us in Argos, and at last
After its huge flight — the flame descended
Direct from the flames of Troy —
Alit here, on the roof of this palace.
This was the relay race of my torchbearers.
And this is my proof — this flame. Sent to me
Straight from burning Troy by Agamemnon.

CHORUS

The gods have to be thanked.
But can the flame say more?
How has the war ended?

CLYTEMNESTRA

The Greek army has taken Troy
And now they are shaking it empty.
Troy's famous ring of walls, that kept her so safe,
Has become the closed vessel
Of a cauldron, seething with screams,
With bursts of foaming blood, with tossing bodies,
Severed limbs, heads, chunks, gobbets.
The death-screams of the butchered,
The screams of those about to be butchered
Hunted by bellowing shouts
Down the narrow streets and steep alleys
Into the twists of their burrows.
The happiest day and the worst moment
Collide and grapple, on skidding feet,
In the uproar of a slaughterhouse. The women of Troy
Are a population of mourners.
The men of Troy are a litter of corpses,
Rubbish-heaps of corpses. Troy on its hill
Cascades with blood, as under a downpour
Of bodies from the heavens,
Shattered and entangled with each other
In every passage — mutilations,
Amputations, eviscerations. The women
Are kneeling, shoulders heaving, with eyes hidden,
Over what were yesterday
Husbands, fathers, sons.
They labour at a grief that is already
The first labour of slaves.
And now the conquerors —
Our husbands, our fathers, our sons —
After a night of plundering and savaging
Whatever can be plundered or savaged,
Ravenous for breakfast, gorge among dead hosts.
The war is over. Discipline is over.
Now each man makes his own laws
Out of his own luck.
Warm in blankets, no longer in the dews and the frost,

Weary with slaughter
They sleep in the beds
Of the families they have slaughtered.
After ten years of guarding their backs and their fronts
They close their eyes and relax.
But now let them take care
To respect the gods of that city.
So long as they violate nothing sacred,
Violate no temple, shrine, priest
Or priestess,
Perhaps these destroyers of a city
Will escape destruction.

It is tempting
For the winner, who might have lost his life,
To take all.
And to destroy whatever cannot be taken.
Let us pray they restrain themselves.
They will need the favour of the gods.
It's a long way home—and danger the whole way.
The dead will have many an opportunity
To avenge themselves in full
On those who have angered the gods.

I speak as a woman, hear me:
Let the cycle of killing end here.
Murder for murder, evil for evil:
Let this be the end of it.
And let our hope succeed. I have great hope.

(Exit Clytemnestra.)

CHORUS

She speaks like a man.
We have proof enough
To thank the gods.
At last, we can rejoice.
Zeus, high God,

With the help of darkness
You trawled your net
Through Troy's deep ashes
And lifted it full
Of slaves and plunder.

Zeus, keeper
Of the sacred bond,
Binds host and guest.
You drew your bow
To the tenth long year
Of justice and nailed
Paris to the earth.

So heaven strikes.
Zeus is patient—
His law is obscure,
Roundabout, but
None can escape it.

Let nobody tell you
Heaven ignores
The desecrator
Who mocks and defiles
The holy things—

For they are wrong.
Everywhere
The conceited man
With his lofty scheme
Ruins himself
And everybody near him.

The house where wealth
Cracks the foundations
With its sheer weight
Is a prison

Whose owner dies
In solitary.

What is enough?
Who knows? Once
A man in the stupor
Of wealth and pride
Has broken heaven's law
And kicked over
The altar of justice
It is too late.

Voluptuous promises,
Crystalline logic,
Caressing assurances
Lead him, the slave
Of his own destruction.

While guilt burns
Like a fixed star
The sleepless man
Feels his blood
And the light of his eye
Drained, and replaced
By a kind of filth.

Running after pleasure,
Thoughtless, careless
As a boy
Chasing a bird.
He ruins his people.
He prays, but the gods
Are bedrock rock.
And men who pity him
Share his fate.

So Paris came,
Light-hearted, a guest

Honoured at the table
Of Menelaus—
And in contempt
Of the house of Atreus
And heaven's law
Stole his host's wife.

The light-footed Helen
Flitted with Paris.
She left in Argos
A thunder of anger,
Hammering of bronze,
Assembling of ships,
And took to Troy
Her terrible dowry—
Annihilation.

Menelaus went mad.
He lay on their bed—
A man in a trance.
His soul fluttered
Above the Aegean.
Sleeping, he shouted—
Tortured by dreams.
She was running away
With laughing Paris.
She lay there, laughing
With laughing Paris.
King Menelaus
Cried through the nights
Like a lost child.

And woke to be tortured
By her statue—
Her painted eyes
That stared at him
From a stone body.

So much for the grief of our greatest house.
But he who sailed for Troy with all our men
Left a grief behind him that crushed Argos—
The men who had gone with him began to come back.

They came back
To widows,
To fatherless children,
To screams, to sobbing.
The men came back
As little clay jars
Full of sharp cinders.

War is a pawnbroker—not of your treasures
But of the lives of your men. Not of gold but of corpses.
Give your man to the war-god and you get ashes.
Your hero's exact worth—in the coinage of war.

Such a great hero—he made just this much slag.
Then the widows weep face-eating acid.
The house of Atreus has ruined their houses.
The King cashed in their men—and bought a whore.
The gusty wind
On the plains of Troy
Has torn the voices
Out of their chests
And scattered like smoke
The shapes of their faces
And puffed them inland
To cool Helen.

Now throughout Argos
The mourning for the slain
Gathers like a curse.
Rulers should fear,
Above all, one thing:
The gathering curse
Of their own people.

It curdles the daylight
Thick as a darkness —
A fear in the air.
A weight you can feel
And have to bear.

That leader who herds
His people en masse
Into glorious graves —
Let him be sure:
Heaven is watching.
When his high hand
Unbalances justice
The Furies wake up.
That man strides
Assured and proud
Into the abyss.

Lightning strikes at summits, it shatters high crags.
Men sack cities, are dragged into slavery, are killed.
But the wise live out their days in freedom, quietly.

*(Shouting of women. Some of the Chorus
go out, then return.)*

CHORUS I

Those fires have set the whole city
Ablaze with rumour.
Is there any truth in it
Or are the gods making mischief?

CHORUS II

Never believe news. Those flames are liars.
Open ears make weeping eyes.

CHORUS III

Women let every rumour change their blood —
Then swear it's a fact, and act on it.

CHORUS IV

Women are too like wax. Too easily softened, too easily
  melted.
They have poured themselves into these flames.

(Exit Chorus.)

INTERVAL

(Enter Chorus.)

CHORUS

We shall soon know whether those beacons
Converted the whole of Argos
To a land of dazed fools and sleepwalkers.
Here's a herald, coming in a hurry—
Ragged, battle-stained,
But he's wearing the olive wreath.
Now for the truth—
Not a mouthful of flames and beacons
But the plain words of an eyewitness—
Whether we like them or not.
Let's hope he confirms the flames and beacons.
Whoever hopes for something else—
May they pay the price.

(Enter Herald.)

HERALD

At last I stand on the land where I was born.
Today's sun has lifted me out of the East
And brought me home. After ten years.
The one hope that matters has come true.
The unlikeliest of my hopes—to die at home.
Argos, the sunlight of Argos.
Where Zeus is the Father,

Where Apollo is the healer.
You bent your bow against us, Apollo,
Under the walls of Troy—
Now be our uplift and healer.
And Hermes, god of heralds.
And you, old heroes, who blessed us
When we set out in our strength.
Bless all of us who survived
The storms of hurtling bronze.
You palaces, you walls, thrones and altars,
You Gods, facing the sunrise
With the dazzle in your eyes,
Welcome the creation
Of a new splendour—
Welcome Agamemnon, the King
To every one of us.
He brings a great flame of light—
Out of the darkness.
Zeus set Agamemnon's hand to the plough
That has toppled Troy roots upward.
Her towers rubble, her territory flayed
And gutted. Her people
Either stinking offal, or weeping slaves
Bringing their treasures for tribute.
Between his finger and thumb
Agamemnon, son of Atreus,
Has crumbled the city of Troy
Like dry tinder.
And now he returns, the conqueror,
To claim his honours.

CHORUS
Welcome this man, herald of the Greek army,
Herald of the fall of Troy.

HERALD
Ten years I have prayed to live—for this moment
When I could happily die.

CHORUS

Homesickness tortured you.

HERALD

My tears now are for joy.

CHORUS

Your misery was half-happy.

HERALD

How — half-happy?

CHORUS

You needed your home.
But your home needed you.

HERALD

Argos needed us?

CHORUS

Our need was a misery.

HERALD

What threatened you? Who?
Did any oppress you, or attack you?

CHORUS

Long ago we learned to keep our mouths shut.
Where silence is good health, speech can be fatal.

HERALD

Who troubled Argos
In the King's absence?

CHORUS

You have told us how death here would be welcome.
You could be speaking for us — death would be welcome.

HERALD

Our huge task is done.
All as we wished it.
Yet what did it amount to?
Time scrambles the memory.
Good and evil
Were there in plenty.
The gods can be happy
For a thousand lifetimes.
Suffering belongs
To the days of man.
We suffered in the ships, tortured by boredom and lice,
By the stench, sodden with sweat, vomit, urine—
Sleep a cramp of agony, tumbled in storms—
And on land the dog-holes were worse.
The stench, the rats, the cockroaches, worse.
Filthy with flies and dysentery,
Crutches raw and bleeding, we dug in
Under the enemy's wall. We lived there
Pelted with their ordure,
Or made our beds in the salt marsh
With the crabs and mosquitoes.
Our finger-joints clubbed with rheumatism,
Icy or streaming with fever.
In every ten men, nine were trembling.
Then, God help us, the winter.
The wind off those white peaks.
Toes fell off, birds dropped out of the trees.
A man's back could snap if he bent of a sudden.
Then in midsummer the heat—the heat!
The sea was a puddle of lead.
The earth too hot for the bare footsole.
The touch of bronze blistered.

Thank God it's all over.
No point bemoaning it.
And the dead we left out there, they rest easy.
No need to fret about them.

No point trying to reckon their pain.
Their pain is all spent—all gone.
They're free of it and so are we.
Our past is done with.
The evil that we've suffered no longer exists.
All we have is life—and a future.
These exist—and are good.
Also, if we are wise, we'll stay humble.

One thing we can say:
Great Argos has destroyed the city of Troy
And the spoils of Troy's palaces are trophies
Over the altars of the gods of Hellas.

So give our returning veterans
Feasts and embraces
And give our conquering general a thunder of thanks,
But first and last
Let us remember God, who gives justice.

CHORUS
I am glad to learn I was wrong.
The old who can learn are still young.
Bring this news to Clytemnestra—
This news is for her, she has lived for it.
I am happy simply to overhear it.

(Enter Clytemnestra.)

CLYTEMNESTRA
I started my rejoicing for this victory
When the flames of Troy's blaze jumped half the world
To let me see it. I was laughed at.
Men jeered at a credulous woman.
They went off, shaking their beards.
'Typical inflammable woman.
One spark off a beacon, and Troy is in ashes.'
As if I were some fool.

Yet I went ahead.
I sacrificed, I gave thanks to the gods.
And all Argos was with me—
Women believed me, they crowded the temples.
The shout of triumph went up out of Argos
As thunder came down from the sky.
The land reeked with the smell of burning hair
And sacrificed oils.
Don't bother to give me your herald's official details—
I shall have the whole thing from the mouth of
    Agamemnon.
No woman knows a day sweeter
Than this day—when she opens her arms
To clasp her smiling husband
Brought back from a war by the hand of God.
But first—prepare his welcome,
Take him this message.
Argos loves him.
His wife waits for him here
And she loves him
As when he sailed—
As true to him as the great dog
That guards his door
To savage the trespasser—
Faithful only
To the one master.
His treasures untouched.
His Queen untouched
By any man,
Fingered by scandal
No more than a woman
Would wear weapons.

(*She goes.*)

HERALD

Are such words necessary?
A Queen boasting so strangely?

Why should she trouble us
With such denials?

CHORUS

To a clear understanding her words are clear.
But what about the brother of Agamemnon?
The great King Menelaus? Is he home? Is he safe?

HERALD

I cannot lie to please you.
The pleasure would be brief.

CHORUS

A lie sweet in the mouth is sour in the stomach.

HERALD

The truth is: Menelaus
Has vanished off the earth's face.
And his ship's gone with him.

CHORUS

You mean he sailed with you from the shore of Troy?
Then a storm came—and you lost him?

HERALD

For that word 'storm' understand—'chaos.'

CHORUS

Is he given up for lost, or is there hope?

HERALD

Maybe the sun knows.
But the seabed is dark.

CHORUS

I suspect you are telling us—heaven was angry.
Are you saying our fleet had to be punished?

HERALD

This is no day to count out sorrows.
It's a day for thanking the gods.
I haven't arrived with bulging eyes
Terrified by what I have to tell you
Of a landscape astounding with heaped corpses,
Your army—vistas of putrefaction.
Your every loved one—
Melted into a million flies.
Your tribe's losses already a legend.
If this is what I had to tell you—
Then we could talk of the Furies,
But I bring Victory,
The word of jubilation throughout Argos.
A word like a drug, that maddens with joy.
How can I pollute such a moment
With evil reminders?
Why should I tell
How fate combined with the gods
In a pitiless alliance
Of water and fire?
How those two ancient enemies
Joined their forces to destroy us?
How they came down on us
The moment we left Troy?
How they swore oaths to each other
To exterminate us?

One night the sea heaved
Under a gale out of Thrace.
The sky was a shepherd gone crazy—
Driving his flocks over a great cliff
Into an ocean tempest.
Mountains raced under the miles of swell.
A hurricane skinned the sea,
Lifted it and folded it over.
Our ships mounted each other
In the tumbling tons of foam.

They broke up, turned turtle, were there and were
    gone.
Dawn came windless over an oily calm.
The sun rose on an ocean clogged with wreckage
And bodies of men.
And there, in the thick of it all, we sat afloat.
Only a god's help could have got us through it.
Some god had done a deal.
Our ship had been saved for something.
We were still dazed, we had seen the bottom of the sea.
We stank of our nightlong terror, we were weak with
    retching.

We could only think
Every other ship had gone down
Or had been blown into some other sea.
If any survived anywhere—they'd be thinking
We could never have survived.
But we had, and maybe others were as lucky.
Maybe Menelaus was as lucky.
We have to believe he was lucky. So
As sure as I am here there is real hope
That the sun can see him,
That he can see his own shadow moving.
There's hope too
That God's hatred against this house
Is not absolute. Bad as things are,
That's the truth—and in it there's room for hope.

CHORUS

A woman did all this. One woman.
They called her Helen—that was a prophecy.
Helen the Destroyer.
Not a name but a title.
The bride of the spear's broad blade.
Helen the homicidal
Epidemic fury
That would possess nations.

Not a face or name but a poison
To send whole fleets to perdition
As if their captains were madmen—
Chewing and spitting her name—
Helen. The name Helen
Not so much a name as an earthquake
To bounce a city to burning rubble.
Not a name but a plague.
Spreading scream by scream from city to city,
As houses become tombs.

She left like a breath of perfume
Lifting a curtain—
She went over the sea with the whisper
Of a bird's wing—
One of a pair, skimming the water.
She was followed by shouting thousands,
Heavy with weapons,
A raging hunt, their pack of diviners
Sniffing her out—
Their keels grinding at last in the mouth of Simois.

Troy made a single error.
It forgot the meaning of the word 'pledge.'
It forgot the terrible warriors hidden
In the belly of that word.
It forgot the guarantee of Zeus
In the speaking of that word.
The pledge between guest and host.
The pledge between bride and groom.
Troy married Paris to Helen
And their ignorant marriage songs
Deafened them to those warriors
And the bellowing fury of Zeus
That poured from the word Paris had broken twice.
Deafened them to the screams
That welled up under their singing.
Deafened them to the price

That Troy must pay for Helen—
Helen the Destroyer—
And for the folly of Paris—
The sufferings of Troy, Troy in flames,
Her army massacred—
The very site of the city
Scraped off the earth, and lost.

A farmer took a lion cub home.
He let it suckle milk, with the lambs.
It played with his children, and they cuddled it.
The grandparents smiled to see the cub
Romping among the lambs and the children.
The shepherd nursed the cub in his arms.
It slept in the crook of his arm, or on his knees.
The neighbours laughed and thought it wonderful
To see a lion cub licking the father's face.
But the lion nature could not be hidden.
Time passed, and the day of the lion dawned
Over the farmer's whole family—
The screams and roars went up, and under the doors
Blood came hurrying from the work of the lion.
The high priest of death, at the altar of corpses.

Paris brought Helen.
Her beauty required a new word.
The year, among all its altering moments,
Finds nothing so delicate,
And nowhere such peace.
Among all its medicinal herbs
Nothing so healing.
Among all its blossoms
Nothing like her. Nowhere such sweetness.
But then the fruit came—bitter.
The smiles that had welcomed her to Troy
Contorted in revulsion.
Zeus, protector of the bonds,
Transformed her bridal glance.

It became an arrow—
Fatal for Paris.
And for the city of Troy
A meteorite.

The lucky man's great good fortune
Ruins his children.
This was old wisdom.
Is it true?
Surely the father who breaks heaven's law
Ruins his children.
The father who denies heaven's right
Blinds his children.
The father who forgets to be humble
Crushes his children.
Evil begets evil.
But the children of the man who fears heaven,
They tread with care. They care for the good.
They are rewarded.

Rich pride mounts rich pride
And begets insolence.
Pampered insolence begets
Anarchy.
And anarchy, where every man
Is the tyrant
Of his own conceit,
Begets all-out war—
Striking at heaven and earth.

Justice lives in poverty.
She survives. She measures
What is necessary.
She honours what ought to be honoured.
She seeks out clean hearts, clean hands.
She knows what wealth and power
Grind to dust between them. She knows
Goodness and the laws of heaven.

(Enter Agamemnon with Cassandra, in chariot.
Clytemnestra comes out from the palace to greet him.)

CHORUS

King! Crusher of Troy! King!
What words would be fitting for what you have done?
Flatterers make fools of the flattered.
The world is sick with both.
Some here will smile at you
And hide behind their smiles
Hearts painful with blame.
But you can read their faces,
And weigh the sound of voices.
We all know—
Ten years back when you sailed
And threw all Greece into the scales of the balance
Against a worthless woman—
You were thought to be mad.
And when you made sacrifices
To rid your fleet of a bothersome headwind
And cheer up a demoralised army
Some called it a monstrous act.
But it seemed to work.
Anyway, all that's in the past.
Your victory is ours too.
A good enough end secured
Buys out all the interim that seemed doubtful.
We welcome you, Agamemnon.
Among us, the stay-at-homes,
You will soon sort out those who were loyal—
And the others, you will find them too.

AGAMEMNON

First, let me call on the gods that favour Argos.
You Gods, you shared the revenge I took on Troy.
You Gods, share my triumph.
Heaven heard the prayers of Argos, because they were
    just.

But the prayers of Troy were empty. They were swept up
Like rubbish from the floors of heaven,
And dumped into the pit
As bedding for a slaughtered population—
Where the burial mound, over the mass graves,
Would be the city's ruins. Hope
Gave Troy energy to struggle awhile,
But in the end Troy was suffocated
In the smoke of its own burning wealth.
Troy's luxury glowed into embers of incense,
Mixed with the blue flame of melting corpses.
The smell spread over the sea, to neighbouring lands.
The gods can never be thanked
As they should be thanked.
Let everybody thank them.
Troy raped our woman. Troy no longer exists.
The lion of Argos, ablaze on our shields,
Burst from the belly of a horse, in pitch darkness.
Scattered the bones from the bodies of Troy's heroes,
Lapped up the royal lineage to the last drop
And left the city a bloody stain on the earth.
As for your wise words, I know they are timely.
Not all smiling faces can be trusted.
Envy poisons triumph. Disappointment
Often forges a homicidal hatred.
Kingship has taught me this, like the sting of a
     scorpion:
Life at the top has the best view
Of the depths man will crawl to.
One man alone, of all who were with me,
Odysseus alone, though he hated war
Grudged me nothing of his great heart and his cunning.

We will fix a day for assembly.
I shall need to examine the body of the state.
Wise voices will be valued.
As for the disaffected, no matter who,
And any civil infection, no matter what,

Our surgery shall cut deep.
As we learned at Troy.

But now a prayer to the gods of my own palace:
Here, at the door of my palace, with open arms,
I make my first greeting to the immortals.
You have brought me home in victory.
You protected my going, as for a purpose,
And you have protected my homecoming.
Be with me. And stay with me.

CLYTEMNESTRA

Why should I be ashamed
To let the world hear my love for my husband?
Old men of Argos, you know the childish folly of
    shyness.
I want to cry out what I've learned through ten years of
    bitter waiting.
What revelations I've had while my husband lay
    wrapped in rumours, under the wall of Troy,
Or whirled around the battlefield, embracing his killers
    in a dance of death.
For a woman to sit at home alone while her husband
    flips his life like a coin, heads or tails, in the dust of a
    far-off battle —
Every night an abyss, and every dawn brings dread, an
    anguish deadlier than mourning.
I had to listen to travellers, day after day, darkening the
    house with their latest and worst.
The wounds they gave my husband would have drained
    the whole army.
The deaths they dealt him in their tales would have
    made a mountain of ashes.
They brought despair like a foreign contagion.
Hanging myself was easier, the noose promised a relief
    that sleep denied me — but interfering hands kept me
    alive and waiting for worse.
Do you see why our son Orestes is absent?

Think: if you had been killed—what of him?
Strophius, your faithful friend, he warned me
What would be the fate of Orestes
If you had fallen at Troy. Here in Argos
Conspirators at every street-end—
And behind them the vindictive mob,
Led by the nose. Strophius fosters Orestes.
He is safe in Phocis. And almost a man.

As for me—
I have wept myself dry
As a lump of rubble.
My eyes are raw with staring at the lamp
Night after sleepless night.
Whenever I drowsed, visions of you being butchered
Burst out of the darkness,
Filling my bed with blood.
Nothing is sweeter
Than a safe bay after a tempest.
Or escape from a death sentence,
Only this is sweeter—
To welcome my husband home.
The backbone pillar of this house,
Dearer to me than an only son returning
To his father.
Or a pure spring welling out of the sands
To the thirsty traveller in the desert.
My words could make heaven jealous—
But they surely have been paid for.

Agamemnon, step down from your chariot.
But this bare earth is too poor
For the foot that trod on the neck of Troy.
Hurry—the long carpet of crimson.
Unroll the embroidery
Of vermilion and purple.
The richest silks of Argos are prostrated
To honour the King's tread at his homecoming,

And cushion every footfall of his triumph.
Justice herself shall kiss his instep
And lead him step by step into the home
He never hoped to see.
After this, everything that thinking,
Night after harrowing night,
Hacked out of the darkness,
Everything shall follow
As the immortals have planned.

AGAMEMNON

Guardian of my name, of my home,
Great-hearted woman that you are,
Daughter of Leda—
Your eulogies are like my absence:
Too long, too much.
If I am to be glorified, leave it to others.
Do not bend like a flattering Oriental
To drape my neck with flowery orations.
Do not massage me in public with oiled praise.
And do not spread these purple cloths
That should be spread only for gods,
Yes, only for the feet of gods,
For the feet of descended gods.
Do not spread them for me.
Greet me as a man.
Greet me as a god and the gods
Will punish us all.

True praise needs none of these trimmings.
And the gods' greatest gift
That brings a man to the end of his days in peace
Is a nose to sniff out such imprudence.

CLYTEMNESTRA

Ocean surrounds the earth.
Who can empty the ocean? No mind
Can encompass or fathom the ocean

From which pour the streams of purple dye
To flush our fabrics with all the colours of blood—
Bright scarlet of the lungs,
The liver's deep indigo,
The artery's hot crimson,
Inexhaustible, like life itself
Teeming from the sources in the great deeps.
The gods have been good.
Your treasuries are overflowing
With this kind of wealth.
Even if the oracle had forbidden it
I would have spread twenty times these
If that could have guaranteed
Your safe arrival here,
At the end of your journey.
You are here in your own home—
The hearth of your gods.
The roots of the great tree
That thirsted so long, and were parched,
Can now drink.
Its leaves thicken to shade us
From the burning eye of the sun
And from the Dog-Star's madness.
You have come like a spring day, opening the heart
After locked-up winter.
When Zeus treads the unripe grape
And lets the wine flood out
Then the whole house is blessed.
As it is now
When you step through your own doorway.

AGAMEMNON

This is not for me. My heart throbs
With foreboding.

CLYTEMNESTRA

This could have been your promise
To the gods.

You could have sworn
To enter your home, treading these cloths
In their honour
If only they would bring you safely
Out of some desperate corner,
Some trap where death seemed certain. In that moment
You might easily have promised your rescuers
Such a splendour.

AGAMEMNON
I might. If some holy man had approved it.

CLYTEMNESTRA
And if the gods had let you die there —
If they had thrown you down
To be mutilated and shamed
By some warrior of Priam's —
How would Priam have celebrated that?
Wouldn't he have spread these cloths
To carpet his triumph —
To make it worthy of the gods who gave it?

AGAMEMNON
I have no doubt he would.

CLYTEMNESTRA
You dare not take possession of your triumph
Or act like the conqueror you are.
You are afraid of the rabble's disapproval.

AGAMEMNON
Do you mean the rabble or the people?

CLYTEMNESTRA
No man can be a winner on this earth
Without being cursed by the envy of the rest.
The courage to win is the courage to face envy.

AGAMEMNON

A woman who fears nothing—is she a woman?

CLYTEMNESTRA

What can you fear? You are the absolute conqueror.
Surrender just a little—for me.

AGAMEMNON

So this is a contest—which you need to win.

CLYTEMNESTRA

You have your victory—let me have mine.

AGAMEMNON

How determined you are.
Here—unlace these leathers
That have trampled the walls of Troy.
When I tread this ocean purple
As if the glory were mine
Let no god resent it, or be offended,
As it offends me
To trample such richness under my unwashed feet.
Woven fibres, costly as wire of silver.
This heaped-up, spilled-out wealth of my own house.
Do I make too much of it?

This is Cassandra.
Let her be cared for.
The gods reward a conqueror's mercy.
Her house is ashes, her family is ashes,
And she is now a slave. Treat her as mine.
The jewel of Troy, my army's gift to me.
And now since you have conquered me in this matter
Of treading the crimson path—
Let me enter my house at last.

(He goes into palace.)

CLYTEMNESTRA (*Cries loudly*)
O Zeus! O Zeus!
You who bring everything to fulfilment—
Now fulfil my prayers.
Let me perform your will, let me fulfil it.

CHORUS
A dark weight in the air.
I am suffocating.
My heart labours and staggers.
My blood has thickened.
Some horror is close. Some evil
Settling cold on the skin.
Knowledge of it
Is weakening my whole body.
I cannot argue it away, or escape it.
Common sense, plain reason
Cannot get oxygen.
Trying to wake up
In the waking nightmare, I cannot wake up.
I am still sleepwalking in it.
I knew it before.
The moment the fleet
Up-anchored and sailed
From smouldering Troy
I knew it.
But now the fleet's home
The knowledge has darkened.
The spirit sees many things
But everything goes dark
When the body,
Stupefied by dread, hears the tread
Of the coming fury
With the weapon
That will scatter the purple,
Send the brain spinning
And chop up the shivering nerves
With truth's pitiless edge.

We can pray
To be wrong.
Pray
That these fears are mistaken.
Men talk of good fortune —
We think her a happy bride.
But she is always pregnant
With her own assassin.
And success
Goes blind of a sudden
As it strides
Past the winning post,
And the cry of triumph
Compounds a debt already crippling.

Nevertheless, the ship in a storm,
Foundering and powerless,
Can save itself —
It can dump its cargo
As a tithe,
An offering.
There is hope.

The house that offers the surplus of its wealth
To the gods, the jealous, the dangerous gods,
Will surely buy them off —
Zeus will protect that house.
He will bless its crops and its herds.
Famine — the first and last terror —
Will not come near that house.

But when a man's blood is on the ground,
When its flow pulses
Searching in the dust —
What magic or prayer
Can put it back in the artery
Or brighten the eye dulled in death?

Zeus executed
The healer
Who could resurrect the dead.
That was wise.
That gave man's life a value.
What is a life on earth worth?
What must a murderer
Pay for a human life
That cannot be brought back?
But I know the power of the bond
Between cause and effect. And I know
That the obscure logic of God
Is inexorable.
For taking human life there is a payment
That has to be paid.
If it were otherwise
I would find words now
For what I dare not think.
All these mutterings of mine
Are groans, twisted this way and that.
They are wrung from me with torture—
This dumb fire I hide
That eats my entrails
With knowledge of what is coming.

CLYTEMNESTRA

Cassandra! Come in.
You too have to be cleansed
In the ritual bath.
Come down from that chariot.
It is too late now to be proud.
Zeus is happy
To welcome you to this house.
Among the slave-girls.
Come, and be washed at the altar.
Now it is your fate
To be enslaved.
You are lucky—

This great house knows how to treat slaves well.
It's the newly rich, the upstarts
That are cruel to slaves.
Here you can be sure you will receive
The customary treatment.
Yes, and more.

CHORUS

Cassandra—do you hear Clytemnestra?
She is speaking to you.
Now you're helpless, she's your master.
Can't you understand
Or are you being stubborn?
It's no good, Cassandra, you have to obey.

CLYTEMNESTRA

Is the girl crazed with shock?
Or grief? Or is she an idiot?
Or is she locked up
In some twittering language
Like a strange bird, brought in a cage?

CHORUS

Cassandra—listen.
It's all for the best.
You must obey.
Get down. Go in.

CLYTEMNESTRA

I cannot stand here
Waiting for her to come to her senses.
The sacrificial victims
Are ready at the altar.
If you understand what I am saying:
Come in, now.
Is she deaf and dumb? Make her understand.
Don't stare at me.
Don't think you can make a fool of me.

CHORUS

Who can interpret for her? Look at her —
Like a wild bird trapped in a net.

CLYTEMNESTRA

She's mad, I think.
Her head's tangled and wrapped in her madness.
Her brains are like her father's city —
Ruins and smoking embers, and the stink of corpses.
She's like a mad horse —
She'll not recognise a master
Till all that fury's boiled from her jaws
In bloody froth.

(She goes.)

CHORUS

No, the girl needs pity.
And I pity her.
Step down, you unhappy child.
There's no other way.
Bow your head
To the yoke of necessity.
You have to accept this.

CASSANDRA

Apollo!
No!
O Earth! Earth!
No! No!

CHORUS

You cannot scream at Apollo!
Apollo turns his face from despair.
His ears are closed to the shriek of despair.

CASSANDRA

Apollo! Earth! Oh
No. No. No. Apollo!

CHORUS

Blasphemy!
You cannot defile the name of Apollo
With a voice of such agony.
He hates cries that surrender
To anguish and despair.

CASSANDRA

Apollo! God of my guidance—
You led me the whole long way
Only to destroy me.

CHORUS

It's the prophetic frenzy.
She sees through her slavery and her sorrows
Into the future.

CASSANDRA

Apollo! God of my guidance—
What dreadful place have you brought me to?

CHORUS

Can't prophecy recognise
The house of Atreus?
This is the house of Atreus—
That much is the truth.

CASSANDRA

A house that hates God.
A house that God hates.
Walls weeping blood
Housing butchered innocents,
The blood and the bones of children.

CHORUS

She has picked up the scent
Like a hound.
She's running on the trail splashed with blood—

CASSANDRA

Running in blood. Look —
Look — the witnesses:
Children covering their eyes,
Sobbing blood through their fingers,
Children chopped up, screaming
And roasted and eaten
By their own father.

CHORUS

We don't need a prophet
To tell us this story.

CASSANDRA

Look there. Now. A heart pounding
Thick with hatred
Behind that door. Evil
Is pouring out evil. Blood
Pours out of a body
That expected love.
Taken by surprise,
Naked, helpless —
Bound in the net of pitiless Fate
And coming through the meshes, the blade
Again and again.

CHORUS

That first vision of yours was common knowledge.
What you see now is pitch darkness.

CASSANDRA

She is washing her husband
In his own blood.
He reaches from the bath for her hand
As it jerks him into pitch darkness.

CHORUS

What is she talking about?
Who can unravel this?

CASSANDRA

Now the net—the fish-eye terror:
Death is bundling him up, like a mother
Swaddling a child.
The woman who shared his bed
Is driving the bronze through him.
The Furies crowd into the house
Gorged with the blood of this house,
Ravenous for the blood of this house—
Look at the Furies. Look—look—

CHORUS

Her vision is killing her too.
What are you conjuring up?
It's some kind of death-seizure.
She has to die a little, to see beyond life.

CASSANDRA

Oh!
The cow has gored the great bull.
And it's too late.
He thought it was his robe, it's the mesh of his death.
And the long horn's gone in.
And again. And again. He's wallowing
In a bath full of his own blood.

CHORUS

Oracles need an expert.
I know they always bring evil
And prophets love to make folk tremble and cry.
But what she says terrifies me.

CASSANDRA

And I am there with him.
Look at me—like a dolphin split open
From end to end.
I roll in his blood.
Carved by the same blade.

Apollo—
Why have you tangled me in this man's
Horrible death?

CHORUS

Possessed by the god, crazed—
Yes, lamenting her own death.
She's the nightingale, squealing
And choking on her own history.

CASSANDRA

The bird can fly
But I have to go down
Under the hammer-blow
That will empty me—
Like a chicken on a block.

CHORUS

Where is it coming from?
This outpouring of evil.
This lava-flow of blood and stifling sulphur,
Mouthings about God and all meaningless.
And that voice out of the middle of the earth
Making my bowels writhe and knot.
Where is it all pointing?
What is happening?

CASSANDRA

Paris with his great love
Annihilated
His own family and his own city.
I grew by Scamander, happy.
That sweet stream.
But now the rivers of the land of the dead
Will flow with my prophecies.

CHORUS

We know what Paris did.
But what do you mean by the rest of it?

What she says
Is the thorn-scratch of a snake's fang
That hits the whole body like a dull club.

CASSANDRA

Nothing could block the flight of my prophecy.
Troy's walls were not enough.
Her towers not enough.
The beasts slaughtered daily on every altar
Not enough.
Prayers, shields and the strong warriors behind them—
None of them were enough
To deflect my prophecy.
Nobody believed me.
Now they are all dead.
And soon I shall be with them.

CHORUS

Clear vision, dark speech.
What monstrous reality
Is pushing to be born
Through that tormented mouth?

CASSANDRA

You want to know?
I'll rip away these bridal veils
Where prophecy peeped and murmured.
I'll let it go, like a sea-squall
That heaps the ocean and piles towers
Of thunder into the sunrise—
I'll bring out a crime
More terrible than my own murdered body
Into the glare of the sun.
No more mystery. I will show you
How far back
The track of blood and bloody guilt
Began, that now sets me
And Agamemnon and Clytemnestra

Face to face today.
This house is full of demons.
The loathsome retinue
Of the royal blood.
Under these painted ceilings they flitter and jabber.
They huddle on every stair.
They laugh and rustle and whisper
Inside the walls.
They shift things, in darkness
They squabble and scream in the cellars.
And they sing madness
Into the royal ears. Madness.
Till royal brother defiles the bed of his brother.
Did that happen?
The foundations of the house of Atreus
Split open when it happened,
And the evil poured out, up and out.
Isn't that true? Swear it's true.

CHORUS
Oaths can't improve the truth.
But how do you know all this?

CASSANDRA
This is Apollo's gift of the spirit.

CHORUS
We have heard the god lusted for your body.

CASSANDRA
Too late now for shame. Yes, he did.

CHORUS
When there's hope ahead, we keep our secrets.

CASSANDRA
He pressed me hard and hot as a god can.

CHORUS

What was the upshot of it? A child?

CASSANDRA

I promised he could have me—then denied him.

CHORUS

But weren't you already a famous prophet?

CASSANDRA

Yes, I had prophesied the fall of Troy—
The fall of my own city.

CHORUS

How did Apollo vent his disappointment?

CASSANDRA

Nobody would believe my prophecies.

CHORUS

We believe every word you say.

CASSANDRA

Ah!
Perfect vision is agony.
Hideous things, the brain crammed
With unbearable things.
Look at them, sitting on the wall—
Children, cradling the bundles of their own butchered
    bodies—
Butchered by their own families.
Look—
They hold out their own hearts and livers.
Rib-cutlets, haunch and saddle—
Just as their father ate them,
Tore the meat from the bone and washed it down with
    gulps of wine

As he reached for more.
This crime still has to be paid for.
There's a lion in this palace,
A cowardly lion
Plotting the death of the great King
Whose bed he lolled in for years.
While the great King crushed the city of Troy.
When the King returned
The houndbitch licked his hand,
The cowardly lion and the houndbitch
Fawned and bowed in the dance of their plot.
And the King sees nothing of the avenger
Staring through her smile,
Opening beneath his feet—
Dark as blood, bottomless as death.
He does not see
The great wound swimming upwards
Towards him, from the depths of the bath
As his wife, the man-killer, kisses him,
The woman with the heart of a demon.
Is there a name for her—
Basilisk, with her fatal, piercing glare,
Dog-headed, man-eating sea-monster,
Shark ripping from beneath.
All she ever dreams is the broad blade
Going into her husband's body.
You heard her scream of triumph
When she heard he was home?
She made it sound like joy for his victory.
You don't believe me?
No matter. What is coming will come.
And you will have to watch it.
Then you will pity me.

CHORUS

We know how Thyestes ate his children.
And it horrifies us.
But not more than the truth of your vision of it

Astounds us.
The rest of what you say—
What are we to make of it? What does it mean?

CASSANDRA

It means the dead body of Agamemnon.

CHORUS

Are you mad? Those words should never be
   pronounced.

CASSANDRA

My silence cannot keep his body alive.

CHORUS

If the gods can hear us he will live.

CASSANDRA

Pray for him if you like—while others kill him.

CHORUS

No man would dip his hand in such pollution.

CASSANDRA

Man, do you say? Did you hear my prophecy?

CHORUS

Such a plot in this palace? Impossible!

CASSANDRA

My Greek is clear but still no one believes it.

CHORUS

All oracles speak Greek and all darkly.

CASSANDRA

Apollo! I can feel
The shock waves of my own death

Coming towards me.
Apollo, snatch me away somehow.
This lion-woman who coupled with a wolf
In her lord's absence—
She will kill me. She has whetted the bronze.
Like a witch mashing her herbs,
She swears to make her husband's brain whirl,
Pouring my blood into his,
Stirring our blood together in the same vat—
Corpses together since we arrived together.

This garb is ridiculous on me—
This prophet's robe
Wrapping me in my own dissolution,
This staff, and these garlands—
They bring me my own death—
Get away from me.
I curse you as you have cursed me.
Trampling these, I feel some freedom
From the curse of my life.
Let Apollo look at this.
Go, give some other foolish woman
The glorious gift of misery.
It made the god happy
To see me laughed at and jeered at,
Mocked as a gypsy, a frightener,
Some hysterical actress with a mad whisper,
A brain-damaged girl, hallucinating.
A pitiable deluded pest at the feast,
Dolled up in this occult regalia
Bestowed by Apollo.
I bore all this derision.
And now Apollo,
Who gave me this one painful sparkle
Of his own huge blaze of foreknowledge,
Trips me up, in a twist of history,
Into this abattoir, pushes me sprawling

To vomit his gift
Here on these bloody floors—
My last gasp of the incredible.
This is where disbelief will finally desert me.
No longer a mocked seer
Pitied at my father's hearth—
But a carcase chopped on a block,
A butcher's block already oily and warm.
But the gods watch these deaths,
They are sending one to avenge us.
A true son of his father's justice
Who will punish his mother.
Now an exile blowing in the wind,
He will put the topmost stone
On this family's monument
Of bloody crime.

The gods have sealed the contract
That binds the son of Agamemnon
To get the full price
For his father's carcase.

I've finished with tears.
Finished with prophecy
And the pitiless designs of fate.
Finished with Troy
And the will of the gods.
Death is my new life.
Let me welcome it.
No struggle or clinging to breath and tears—
A single numbing blow to liberate me.
Then let me drop and relax and melt
Into the huge ease—of death.

CHORUS

Suffering and wisdom together
Have given you sight

To pierce through the earth.
But seeing your death
As if you had undergone it
And come back to tell us—
How can you return, now,
So calmly
Towards the stroke
Too heavy to bear?

CASSANDRA

What must happen
Has already happened.

CHORUS

But our whole life
Is a deferment.

CASSANDRA

Life too runs out.

CHORUS

Now we see courage.

CASSANDRA

Praise for the wretched.

CHORUS

One brave death
Helps many living.

CASSANDRA

O my father! My brothers!
My death, too, is useless to you.

(She goes in, but recoils, screaming.)

CHORUS

What have you seen?
Worse than your vision of it.

CASSANDRA

The floors are washed with blood.

CHORUS

The sacrifices have begun, they are blessings.

CASSANDRA

The whole palace
Reeks like a mass grave dug open.

CHORUS

You mistake the perfumes scattered for the banquet.

CASSANDRA

I'm not a bird
Scared by the shaking of a leaf.
You are my witnesses.
When you see my killing paid for
With the killing of a woman,
When you see a man killed
To pay for the man
Killed by his smiling wife
Then let it be known—
My prophecies were all true.
I make this request
Before I die.

CHORUS

How horrible to foresee death so clearly.

CASSANDRA

A last word.
A lament, a prophecy, a prayer.
You, sun in heaven,
The last light on my face—
Look down on all this
When the avenger's weapon
Exacts the full price for Agamemnon

Drop for costly drop
From his murderer's veins,
Let him remember the blood
Emptied from my chained, slave body—
Let that too be paid for.

This was life.
The luckiest hours
Like scribbles in chalk
On a slate in a classroom.
We stare
And try to understand them.
Then luck turns its back—
And everything's wiped out.
Joy was not less pathetic
Than the worst grief.

(She goes in.)

CHORUS

No man has enough luck.
While envy dreams bitterly
Of that man's overflowing blessings
He knows what he lacks.
He too dreams of good fortune
As if she'd rejected him.

The gods gave our King
The prize of Troy.
All Greece rejoices for him.
But now he must bathe and drown
In the blood spilled
By his own forefathers.

And his killers, in their turn,
Will be choked in his blood.
This is how Fate has arranged our existence.

Who on this earth can hope
To find a quiet life
And a name without stain?

(Agamemnon shouts inside palace.)

CHORUS

Whose voice is that? Somebody is being murdered.

AGAMEMNON

Help! Help! They have killed me.

CHORUS

That was a death-cry—
And it was the King.
Quick—what should we do?
We must have a plan.

CHORUS I

The whole city
Ought to assemble instantly
Under arms.

CHORUS II

Too slow and vague.
We should burst in, break open the doors
And catch them in the act.

CHORUS III

Yes—act now.
Some way or other
We must act now.

CHORUS IV

The King assassinated!
Out of every bloody regicide
Steps a tyrant.

CHORUS V

Talk, talk, mutter, mutter.
If we want action
We trample on caution.

CHORUS VI

But what's our plan?
A plan has to be practical.
Oughtn't we to wait
For their next clear step?

CHORUS VII

One thing is certain.
Whatever we do
The King stays dead.

CHORUS VIII

What, live like slaves
Under the feet
Of these gangsters
Just for peace?

CHORUS IX

Better dead
Than have our mouths stopped
By a tyrant's heel.

CHORUS X

We're in too much of a hurry.
We heard the screams for sure.
But is the King dead?

CHORUS

Then it seems agreed?
We make a sober enquiry
About the King's health.

(Corpses revealed.)

CLYTEMNESTRA

You heard me pronounce the words required by the
    moment.
The moment has passed. Those words are meaningless.
How else could I have killed this man—
My deadliest enemy?
Lies and embraces were simply my method.
The knots in the net that enmeshed him.
I pondered this for a long time.
And when the moment for action came
I made no mistake. See, my work
Perfected. I don't disown it.
Every possibility of error
I wrapped in a great net—
Not a fish could have slipped from the shoal.
His struggles merely tightened the tangle.
Then, at my leisure, choosing the best places
On his helpless body
I pushed the blade into him. Once, twice.
Twice he screamed. You heard him.
Then his eyes stared elsewhere.
His body arched like a bow being strung,
Every muscle straining for life.
I placed the point for a third and final time
And drove the blade clean through him.

That was my thanks to God
For fulfilling my prayers.
I offered this murder up
To God—protector of the dead.
Then the blood belched from him with a strange
    barking sound.
A foaming jet that showered the walls
And showered me, like a warm spring rain
That makes the new-sown corn swell with joy
And the buds split into blossom.
I felt my whole body exult.

So there it is, old men of Argos.
Applaud or weep, as you please.
I exult.
He filled the wine-jars of this house
With evil. Not with wine but with blood.
Just as we pour out wine to thank the gods
For the traveller's safe return,
We have poured out the blood
That poisoned this house, poisoned Argos,
And now, as the last dregs of it clot in his beard,
Has poisoned him.

CHORUS

Your words are stupefying.
To rejoice so shamelessly
Over the husband you have just murdered!

CLYTEMNESTRA

You think I'm some irresponsible woman?
You are making a mistake.
My heart and my brain are like this blade,
Bronze, and forged with a purpose.

Here's my husband, Agamemnon,
Dead as the floor that he cannot feel,
And from which he will never get up.
And here is the hand that Justice contracted
To kill him. And it killed him.
Yes, I have killed him.
So there the whole truth lies.

CHORUS

Horrible woman!
Some drug has snarled your brains.
Some viperous root
Has tangled your woman's feeling
Into subhuman knots—
You no longer see

What you have done, no longer feel
The touch of guilt, the hard clutch
Of murder-guilt.
All Argos will vomit this up,
This work of yours
Like poison fungus,
With cries of loathing
They will drive you from Argos—
Outlawed, polluted, accursed.

CLYTEMNESTRA

How ready you are, of a sudden,
To bleat about banishment.
The righteous curse of the public!
The sacred verdict of the mob.
Where were they, and where were you
When this monster here
Butchered his own daughter on the block?
He found it easier
Than sacrificing one of his precious cattle
To butcher my daughter—
Like somebody else's goat.
All to persuade the wind to shift a few points
And make some sailors happy,
He ripped my daughter's throat and shook the blood
   out of her.
To gratify his whimpering love-sick brother
And catch a runaway whore.
Why didn't you judge Agamemnon?
He murdered his own daughter, my daughter,
On the whim of some shivering priest
Who had to come up with something.
This man here was the criminal
To be punished, and banished.
It never occurred to you. Why not?
You were afraid of him.
But now you think you have power
To be righteous.

You think you can handle me.
You have your official law-enforcers
As you think. Let's put it to the test.
Let's see what your power amounts to
When you discover how little power you have.
I shall teach you old men
The lesson you failed to learn when you were children.

CHORUS

Yes, power. It is power that has driven you mad.
Power, and the greed for more power,
Have made your cunning stupid.
As sure as that blood on your gown
Is Agamemnon's, the time is fast coming
When your own blood will join it.
All your silks and finery, on that day,
Will be a sop of purple.
Wait:
Friendless, dishonoured, every man's hand against you,
Wound for wound, you shall pay.

CLYTEMNESTRA

You are forgetting something.
I too can swear a sacred oath—
The gods can hear me too.
By my daughter's protector, Justice,
Here perfected—as you can see,
By Iphigenia, by the Fury
That must avenge her
And has avenged her—that holy Fury
For whom I poured this blood,
I swear by these, I am not afraid
Of this murder's avenger
While my own protector, Aegisthus,
Stands at my hearth beside me.
With such a shield, I feel my strength
And fear nothing.
While this one here, this harvester

Of all Troy's fallen girls
Who trampled out their wine and soured my life,
Lies dead as a gutted fish. Look:
In the majestic face the eyes are empty.
And his trophy, this prophetess—
Who softened his voyage home
And draped his sleeping body with her beauty
And was to have added a charm to my bed—
There she lies, like a dead swan
After its last song—
Like a sculptor's crest
On the monument of my triumph,
Her body on his body
Gaping at the future in the same sink of blood.

CHORUS

He was our King. Our holy leader.
Mourn him. He protected his people.
I could easily die now,
And go with him.
What happens to Argos without him?
If only I could close my eyes and be gone.
Dragged into ten years' war
By one vicious woman, Helen,
Now murdered by another.
Helen, besotted,
Kissed the best of two whole armies
Into their death-convulsion,
Drained the blood from them
To feed the roots
Of the curse
That has split the breast of Agamemnon
And the foundations of this house.

CLYTEMNESTRA

You cannot change what has happened.
Stop whining for death.
And stop blaming Helen

For the annihilation of armies.
As if her little flutter, all on its own,
Could have unloosed
All this misery on so many.

CHORUS

Unfathomable evil! The spirit of evil
Wears the face
Of Clytemnestra—
The curse of Tantalus descends
Generation to generation
To writhe behind your lips.
It forms your words, flares at your eyes
And wields your thoughts.
Like a great bird, a carrion-eater,
It flings your shadow across us.

CLYTEMNESTRA

Then blame the curse. Yes, blame the curse.
The blood-eating Fury
That hates our house.
She tries to slake her thirst and her hatred
In every generation.
And the salt blood of her each feast
Crazes her with a new thirst for the next.

CHORUS

This horror, this evil
You describe so truly
Is insatiable.
Ruin of kings,
Armies, cities
Shines on her lips.
Yet God sends her.
Zeus, creator
Of all things—he
Has appointed her flight path.

Agamemnon is dead.
He was our King.
Argos must mourn him.
When all is said
He was killed
By his treacherous wife.
The spider's web
Swaddled him helpless.
Then a bronze blade
Came out of nowhere.
A great King died
Like a spinning fly.

CLYTEMNESTRA

You say I killed him
And I was his wife.
You saw better
When you saw
The curse, the hideous
Heritage
Of the house of Atreus
Standing here
In my shape.
Yes, that one,
That blood-rotten Fury,
Her mouth stinking
From the first
Ancient crime
Of Atreus,
Still gorged and sick
With the feast he set
In front of his brother.
That Fury, she
Steered the blade
Through Agamemnon,
Not I. Not my hand.
The hand of our daughter

Iphigenia
Steadied the hand
Of that Fury
To empty the blood
From this pair.
On behalf
Of those two children
Stewed in their blood
By Atreus—
And spewed out by his brother
Thyestes.
All these years later
Iphigenia
Forced her father
To lap up that mess—
Off the floor
Of his own house.

CHORUS

You are not guiltless.
Maybe possession
By some supernatural being
Gave you the insane strength.
But you yourself prayed for it.
You sharpened the weapon
As surely as you held it.
The war-god, the death-god,
The god of an outraged pride,
The god of the killing fury
Is inexhaustible.
Like a tidal wave
That swamps harbour cities
He bursts
From the hearts of brothers,
Looking for justice
Through eyes
Blocked
With blood.

Our King's death is pitiable.
Our love comes too late.
He was killed
By his treacherous wife.
The spider's knots
Bound and gagged him—
Then a bronze blade
Came out of nowhere.
Our great King died
Like a spinning fly.

CLYTEMNESTRA

If I was treacherous,
When Agamemnon cursed this house afresh,
Painted the walls with a fresh cast of curse
By killing his own daughter, my daughter,
His treachery was worse.
While I wept myself blind
He closed his eyes.
And the sword he brought down
On the nape of her neck
Severed his own backbone.
The curse he released
From her virgin body
Has washed him to hell.
Let him tell the dead that.
Let him brag in hell
About that.

CHORUS

Where is the right and wrong
In this nightmare?
Each becomes the ghost of the other.
Each is driven mad
By the ghost of the other.
Who can reason it out?
Reason fails, mind is a casualty
Of this bloody succession.

The throne of Argos
Slides on blood, in a tilting house —
Everything rushes
Towards some great scream.
As if Creation itself screamed.
As if Justice herself
Were tearing Creation open.
Better to be dead and out of it.
Earth, you Earth,
Why didn't you take me back,
Wrap me up in your hills
And horizons of infinite quiet,
Before I saw the King's body
Caught in a net like a quail, his neck broken?
Who will bury him?
Will you?
First kill him, then bewail him,
Then heap his tomb with your lies?
What can Justice make of it?
Who will give him the funeral of a great King?

CLYTEMNESTRA

I killed him.
I'll bury him.
There will be no fuss.
No futile, pompous display.
A quiet affair —
And Iphigenia, his beloved daughter
Who died a mere girl,
Will welcome him
To the land of the dead
With a silent kiss.

CHORUS

Revenge begets revenge,
Truth spins and evaporates
As blood drains from the head.

It is the law of Zeus:
A life for a life.
What is a human life worth?
More than itself, more than a life,
Or less? Or precisely the same?
The law of Zeus demands
A life for a life.
All—for all.
But this law of Zeus
Is a kind of disease
Inherited through the blood.
See how it has crazed
Every member of this house.

CLYTEMNESTRA

Now you are beginning to understand.
The murderer must die.
You Powers, whoever you are
That hammer out your remorseless logic
In the heartbeat of this house,
I am satisfied.
Everything that has happened,
Horrible as it is,
I accept.
Now leave us.
All rancour is dead in me.
There is nothing more here
For you to feed on.
This abattoir and hospital of a house
Has to be stripped and cleaned.
Forget us.
Find some other blood-glutted
Family tree of murder—
Go and perform your strange dance
Of justice in their branches.
Leave us.
I ask for nothing,

Now the killing is over—
Only to be left in peace.

(Enter Aegisthus.)

AEGISTHUS

Justice! At last the day of justice has dawned.
This is perfect proof that the gods
Watch men and punish evil.
What a beautiful sight
To see this man gagged and bound
In meshes knotted by the Furies!
To see his body
Emptied of all its blood.
At last he has paid
For the inhuman crime his father committed
Against my father. You should know
His father and my father had quarrelled.
Agamemnon's father, Atreus,
Ruled Argos.
Atreus had driven out of the city
My father, his brother Thyestes.

Thyestes came back.
Forgave, begged to be forgiven,
Sat at the hearth of Atreus, a supplicant,
Happy simply to live in peace with his brother.
Happy simply to live.
Atreus hid his hatred.
He gave my father a banquet.
He took my two brothers,
The two eldest sons of Thyestes,
Cut their throats and bled them,
Butchered them, and stewed the meat.
The feet with their toes, the hands with their fingers
He hid at the bottom of the dish.
Over those he layered the steaks and collops,
The chopped livers and kidneys, the hearts, the brains.

Each guest had a separate table.
This was the dish set steaming before my father.
He had gorged himself, to honour the feast,
Before he discovered what he was swallowing.
When he recognised it,
When he saw the hands and the feet
He fell backwards, vomiting over the floors
His own children.
He kicked the table over, and as the bowl shattered
He screamed out this curse—
To earth and to heaven and to hell he screamed it:
'Just as this bowl shatters
So let the whole lineage of Atreus
Be shattered and spilt.'

That day was fatal to Agamemnon—
As this corpse proves.
I plotted this killing.
In the name of Justice.
I was the third brother—
An exiled babe, nursing my stricken father.
Justice guided my steps a long way round
To this palace,
Carrying the noose in my hands.
Now, seeing justice so perfectly done,
I think I could die happy.

CHORUS
Aegisthus, you have condemned yourself.
If this whole plot was yours
Then your life is the price.
You will be stoned to death
By the people of Argos.

AEGISTHUS
Do I hear mutterings from below the decks—
Do you hear the slaves?

You old men are about to learn something—
And the lesson is going to be hard.
Prison and starvation can work wonders
In cleansing the tongue,
And making the facts plain and visible.
Think of it. Be careful
What you say to the club
That can break your teeth.

CHORUS

Aegisthus, you are a woman.
While the King fought and thousands died
You sprawled on his bed
And polluted his wife,
And when he came back home you made yourself
    scarce.

AEGISTHUS

What you say sounds like a man
About to break down in tears.
Unlike Orpheus
Whose song tamed wolves and lions.
Your yapping pesters our ankles.
It's time you felt the weight of your master.

CHORUS

Your weight! You our master
On the throne of Agamemnon?
Who plotted his murder so coolly,
Then let a woman do it?

AEGISTHUS

It needed a woman. She was my bait.
She lured him into the trap.
Essential to my plot.
How could he have trusted me, knowing our history?
Now his treasury flowing through my hands
Will help the people to love me, and obey me.

But the stubborn ones, the stiff-necked
Will find themselves broken.

You are fearless with us, but you fled and hid
From the eyes of Agamemnon.
You corrupted a woman
To defile the earth
And her family
And her gods, the gods of Argos,
To kill him because you did not dare.
Where is Orestes?
Good fortune, you blessed good fortune,
Guide the feet of Orestes,
Bring his avenging sword
To rid the earth of this pair.
Let him exact the full price
For the life of his father, Agamemnon.

AEGISTHUS
You hear these revolutionary chickens,
This grey-crested embryo
Trying to crack from its egg?
Guards. Finish the killing.

CHORUS
Our swords are ready.
And we are ready
For death and honour.

AEGISTHUS
Death, yes, by all means, yes.
You were praying for death.
Now you can have it.

CLYTEMNESTRA
Stop. Stop.
The killing is over.

Beloved Aegisthus—
We have planted enough
Of this horrible fruit
That bursts on our plates
And soaks us with purple.
The ripening
Of this first crop
Will bring us
More than enough grief.

You elders, be wise.
What had to be done
Is done with.
Destiny cannot be sidestepped.
Her sword
Has gone through me twice.
I am bowed. I accept it.
You too accept it.
Remember how wisdom
Speaks through women.

AEGISTHUS
They cannot get away with it.
I felt their contempt,
You heard their insults.
Will you let them push all that
Back into their scabbards?

CHORUS
No man of Argos will bend his neck to a dog.

AEGISTHUS
But they shall bend their necks to one who will whip
them like dogs.

CHORUS
Orestes! Fate—find Orestes!

AEGISTHUS

No doubt he's chewing the cud of exile somewhere.

CHORUS

While you gorge here on the carcase of Justice —
Fatten while you can.

AEGISTHUS

You fools, these words you're so eager to release
Will return to kill you.

CHORUS

You muck-heap cockerel — even your hen is ashamed of
    you.

CLYTEMNESTRA

Whatever comes from their mouths —
It amounts to nothing.
Their feet are kicking in the air.
You and I, Aegisthus, we are the law.
The lives of all the people of Argos
Dangle on our word.
Whatever word we speak, that is the law.
At last, the throne of Argos is ours.

CHOEPHORI

(Agamemnon's tomb, outside the palace of Argos.
Enter Orestes and Pylades.)

ORESTES

Hermes, you who guide the soul
After death into the underworld.
Son of Zeus, highest of all the gods,
Zeus who rights all wrongs.
Now be your father's son—
Right my wrongs.
Hear my prayer.
I have come home after a long exile
To claim what is mine.
And to do what I must do.
This is my father's grave.
Agamemnon, the great King, lies here.
Hermes, guide my cries to his ghost.

I offer the hair of my head to you, my father.
Cutting off this first lock,
I lay down my childhood.
This second—
This is my grief, my mourning and my oath.
I lay it on your grave.

I was not there when they killed you—
But now I have arrived
To do what must be done.
Who are those women?
Are they coming here?
Mourners in black?
More death, more anguish?
They come this way—
Each one is carrying a jar—
It must be an offering for my father's grave,
A balm for the injured powers of the earth.
And there so visibly

Isolated by her crueller sorrow,
Electra, my sister.

Zeus, O great God,
Let me have revenge for my father.
Grant me only this.
Be with me as I step towards this.

Let us stand aside, Pylades.
I want to hear what these women are up to.
And we may learn more.

(Enter Chorus and Electra.)

CHORUS
We come at the command of Clytemnestra,
To mourn King Agamemnon.
But our own grief makes it easy.
The rips in our skin are fresh—
Through years of anguish our lives
Have been daily self-annihilation.
Misery tears its clothing and its body.
The spirit declares its pain through rending of the flesh.

A shout broke the silence of midnight.
Sleepers awoke and lay in terror.
A dream was bellowing
Through all the rooms of the house
Out of the sleeping throat of Clytemnestra.
Fate used her sleeping mouth
To tell every listener
That the dead are furious
For vengeance
Against the murderers.
So the Queen, detested
By the gods and the dead,
Sent us at first light
To pour out the oil and the wine

Into the earth's lap—
All to appease the Great Mother.
Rich oil and rich wine
Wrung from the terrible heart of Clytemnestra
Which now begins to stagger with fear.
I am afraid of offering these bribes
To the blood
That howls under the dark stones.
What prayers can wash that howl?
Or wash this accursed royal house
That bathes in the putrescence of its murders,
Horrifying the sun and mankind?

Once all proud Argos
Willingly bowed to a monarch
Who had earned his place.
Not any more.
Reverence has drained into the soil
Like the wine of a shattered goblet.
Fear has shattered it. The terror
Has shattered it.
Nothing is admired
But to have great good luck and get away with it.
Whoever can manage that is a god.
But the criminal
Who wraps his head in his good fortune
And takes a little snooze
Can dream sweet dreams only for so long—
The bow, justice,
And the arrow, vengeance,
Surprise him. He wakes just in time
To die transfixed.

Where man's patient mother, this great earth,
Has been force-fed with blood
And again and again force-fed
With unavenged blood—
Her choked uncried cry

Became a curse, that cannot be ignored
And cannot fail.
The virgin, once violated,
Can never be made whole.
All the pure streams flowing from heaven
And pouring through one bath
Can never wash the hands that have dabbled
In blood that is unavenged.

God gave our city to the enemy,
For loot and for massacre.
We who survived our families are slaves.
Only our boiling hatred
Keeps its freedom, under the breastbone.
And our scream against the tyranny
Of this throne, this Queen and her consort,
Gags itself with a fold of cloak.

ELECTRA
Women, you who are bound
To serve the house,
Since you attend me here, too,
At the performing of this rite—
Advise me.
What prayers ought I to pray
With all these gifts for a tomb?
How can any words of mine
Please my murdered father?
Shall I pour the wine out, crying:
'I bring this from your wife, my mother,
Clytemnestra, and I pour it
As a pledge of our love'?
That would need a tongue of bronze.
I cannot pour out the oil,
The wine, the milk, the honey—
And follow the custom
Asking for a blessing on the givers
When I should be asking for justice.

It would be more fitting
If I poured this wealth out in silence
As he poured out his blood, in that silence
After his last cry.
Then I should go, in silence,
As if I had dropped and hidden something vile,
Without looking back.
Friends, we share the misery of the house
And we share a hatred
As if we were links in the one chain.
The gods know our fate—
Whether slave or free
Neither you nor I can choose
Or escape it.
Speak to me openly. Advise me.

CHORUS
By this tomb, which is as sacred to me as any altar,
I will open my heart to you, and hide nothing.

ELECTRA
Let this tomb be our sacred witness. Now speak.

CHORUS
Pour the wine, and pray for those you can trust.

ELECTRA
Those I can trust? Who can I trust?

CHORUS
Yourself. And all who hate Aegisthus.

ELECTRA
For myself. And for you? Shall I make this prayer for
    you?

CHORUS
You know the truth of my words. You decide.

ELECTRA

What other can there be—that I can trust?

CHORUS

Pray for Orestes. Pray for far-off Orestes.

ELECTRA

Orestes! Yes! For Orestes!

CHORUS

And for the murderers pray—

ELECTRA

Yes, pray what?
What shall I pray for the killers? What?

CHORUS

Pray
That a god or a man
May come, bringing justice.

ELECTRA

To judge, to convict, to condemn.

CHORUS

To kill! Blood for blood. Pray for that.

ELECTRA

Can God hear a prayer for assassination?

CHORUS

Evil for evil is justice
And justice is holy.

ELECTRA

O Hermes, messenger of the gods,
Pathfinder and guide of the underworld,
Great go-between above and below, help me.

Speak for me,
Awaken the powers of the dark earth,
Protectors of this house,
Command them to hear me,
And call to the Earth herself,
Call to our Great Mother
Gravid with all life,
Mother of everything, nurse of every plant and creature,
Great womb quickened by mankind's offerings—
Beg her to hear me.

And now I pour out water of purification for my dead
    father—
And I call on his spirit. Father—
Pity your children. Pity me. Pity Orestes.
Pity your son, Orestes, and your daughter.
We are disinherited and homeless,
Bartered by our own mother,
Sold off in exchange for Aegisthus,
Supplanted by your killer.
I live among slaves. I live the life of a slave.
Orestes is banished.
How shall we get our home back?
Aegisthus and your Queen, Clytemnestra,
Glitter among the luxury of your treasures
Like two serpents coiled together
In a gorged sleep.
Father, where is Orestes?
Guide him home.
Hear my prayer and answer it.

All I ask for myself
Is to be unlike my mother—
Hands, heart, thoughts clean,
Unlike my mother,
Conscience clean, undarkened by blood,
Unlike my mother.
These prayers are for us.

Now for our enemies —
Father, your avenger,
Let him come with a blade
Remorseless as the blade they pushed through you.
Let him measure it out, the length and the breadth
Of death for death,
Justice for murder.
What are your murderers hoping for?
Orestes' blade is my hope.
They curse you, and buried their curse to the hilt.
Orestes' blade is my curse.

Father, bless me
With your answer to these prayers —
Let the underworld assent,
Let the gods assent
To justice.
Hear my prayers as I pour out these offerings.
All of you with me, we must awaken the dead.

CHORUS

The sea of tears
That washes Troy
Is bottomless.
Let it wash Argos —
Salt, cold water
Purge the blood
Of Agamemnon.
Our cries
Are bottomless. Out of our eyes
Our tears are bottomless.
Pour them for Agamemnon.

Bring his avenger —
Bring the resolving blade
To cut the heavy
Coagulated

Rope of guilt
That chokes this house,
The strangling cramp
Of the two bodies
Knotted in their crime.
Hack them apart.

ELECTRA

The wine has gone into the grave. My father
Drinks my libation. What is this?

CHORUS

Why did my heart lurch when you picked that up?

ELECTRA

A tress of hair—laid on my father's grave.

CHORUS

Is it the hair of a man or woman? Who
Laid it there?

ELECTRA

Can't you see whose it is?

CHORUS

If you know, tell us. Whose is it?

ELECTRA

No other of Agamemnon's house would have offered it
If not me.

CHORUS

Your mother might have—if she were not his killer.

ELECTRA

Colour, texture, everything about it
As I hold it—all so familiar.

CHORUS

What's so familiar? Whose hair does it resemble?

ELECTRA

Ours. The hair of my family. Mine.

CHORUS

Orestes?

ELECTRA

The hair resembles his.

CHORUS

How could Orestes dare set foot in Argos
To lay this tribute of hair on his father's grave?

ELECTRA

He mourns at a distance. He sent it in secret.

CHORUS

He had to send it. Orestes dare not
Stand in his native land, at his family's tomb.
We shall mourn for this too.

ELECTRA

Mourn? I want bitterness and fury
Like a tidal wave at midnight
To overwhelm me.
Where others feel their heart's pity
I feel a sword-blade, hard-edged.
Out of the huge sudden waves
That tear me adrift
Two droplets
Splashed from my eyes when I saw this.
No other from Argos owned this.
Not that murderess, my mother,
Though it resembles hers.
She laughs at the gods and curses her children.

Nevertheless, my heart struggles—
It faints from the belief
That Orestes,
Dearer to me than this world and the next,
Sent this tress of hair.
Hope flatters fools.
If this hair could speak for itself,
If it could tell me, loud and clear,
That it is Clytemnestra's,
Then I could grind it under my heel.
If it could tell me
That it comes from the head of Orestes,
Then it could bless me, and bless this tomb,
And honour Agamemnon.

The gods who hear us
Know what tempests
Tangle our lives, and bewilder our voyage
In their criss-cross winds.
But if there's a future
A huge tree can tower
From a tiny seed.

Look! Fresh footprints.
Though I have not stepped where they are, they are
Familiar as my own.
Do these footprints belong to the hair?
As like my own as the hair is.
Heel, instep, toes—
My own prints magnified. Oh, let me pray.
My head throbs. I think my heart
Is going to burst.

(Orestes comes forward.)

ORESTES

Your prayers are answered.
Now you can boast

That the great gods
Hear and obey.

ELECTRA

Who are you?
Which of my words have the gods obeyed?

ORESTES

Your oldest prayer—fulfilled this very moment.

ELECTRA

If you know my secret prayer, you know
The name it bears.

ORESTES

Your every heartbeat pronounces a name: Orestes.

ELECTRA

How can that prayer and name ever be more
Than a prayer and a name?

ORESTES

By standing here before you.

ELECTRA

Perhaps like an open trap.

ORESTES

The trap is also trapped.

ELECTRA

Don't play with my pain.

ORESTES

Your pain and mine are one.

ELECTRA

Orestes! Do I call you Orestes?

ORESTES

How slow you are
To see the truth
Where it stands.
When you found this tress
Laid on the grave,
A boy's offering
To his father,
Your heart almost
Leapt from your body
At a vision of my face.
You heard my name
Ringing in the air.
You knew my footprints
And knew them for mine
Better than now
You know my face.
See this—here's
Where the tress belongs.
You see the cut.
Look at this cloak—
Do you recognise
The animals
Your own hands wove
On your own loom?
Electra, master yourself. Keep control
Of the wild joy
That rushes into your body
Like a horse broken loose.
Those closest to us are the cruellest.
Let them know nothing.

CHORUS

Prince Orestes! Most precious of all
Your father's treasures.
The living root of your father's lineage
Fed by grief. Be strong
To reclaim your father's home and his throne.

It is your face, Orestes.
The face of my four joys—
All that remains of our father;
All that remains of our mother—who became
The murderess of our mother
When she murdered our father;
All that remains of our sister,
Iphigenia, sacrificed so lightly
For a puff of air—
Three vessels of love
Poured into you, my fourth,
My brother who has not changed—
Your very name has delivered me
From slavery and shame.
Now let God,
And his justice, give you the prize
Of avenging our father.

ORESTES

Zeus, look down, look at us.
Watch what we do now.
We are the eagle's children,
Bereft, in the nest fouled
With the corpse of an eagle
Tangled in the meshing coils
Of the snake that struck.
See what deprivation
Has done to the helpless,
Strengthless fledgelings—
Yet the eagle's flight,
The eagle's prey, the eagle's nest, the highest eyrie
Belong to us.
Look at us, Zeus. Look at Orestes and Electra,
Orphaned and exiled.
King Agamemnon piled up sacrifices
And poured out libations
In a perpetual banquet

Of offerings to you.
If you let us perish
That banquet is over.
And when the eaglets are dead
How shall men read
Your signals in heaven?
Who will honour
Your unresponsive altars?
Root out this evil monarchy.
Rescue this house.
Lift from its fall
Our tree of strength.
From the King's grave
Let our glory
Rise again.

CHORUS

Not so loud, not so loud.
The air is an ear.
There is no tongue
That can forgo
The pleasant feeling
When another man's secrets
Make us the wonder
Of a stunned listener—
So those tyrants
Would gulp this,
Whom God, in his goodness,
Will give to me, dead,
Their bodies hissing
And cracking in the flames
Like resinous pine.

ORESTES

Apollo's command is like Fate.
No man can refuse it.
The voice of Apollo, relentless,
Directs my feet, my mind, my hand

Towards this collision
Of killer with killer.
The voice of Apollo
Freezes my body
To a lump of ice
Recounting the horrors
Waiting for me
If I fail.
Or if I flinch
Or dodge off sideways
From this task:
'Blood for blood, your face fixed like bronze.'
Their debt cannot be weighed out in gold.
And if I fail, I pay for failure
With my own life.
Apollo
Told me what rites men must perform
To appease angered spirits of the earth.
He told me what their unappeased anger
Spills into men's homes.

The ulcers that gnaw the human shape
To an oozing stump.
The white fungus that flowers on the ulcers.
Then he told me
What the unavenged blood of a murdered father
Presents to the eyes of a negligent son.
The Furies, forcing their way out of thick darkness,
Drunk with the fumes of that blood,
Their arrows flying in the darkness,
Insanity flung like a net,
Their night horrors dragging the sleeper awake,
Hunting him from collapse to deeper collapse,
Lashing him from city to city
With whips of bronze wire—
Befouled in blood and suppuration,
Loathed and shunned as if leprous.

Banished alike from the banquet
And from the sacred precinct.

The voice of the oracle of Apollo
Pronounced all this.
The anger of that man's dead father
Drives him, an outlaw
From temple and from hearth. In the end
Abominated, abandoned, alone
He dies. A shape in some corner,
Like the husk of an insect, hugging the dust,
Mummified by death.
Am I to believe these ghostly words of an oracle — can
    they be trusted?
Even if I reject them, I still have to do what they tell me
    to do.
My motives are many and strong, quite apart from that
    clear command of the great god.
My head pounds with my grief for my father, every beat
    of my heart roars 'vengeance!'
I am sleepless with fury, knowing my whole inheritance
    lies in the blood-fouled hands of Aegisthus.
And I am sick with shame to see the noble people of
    Argos,
Who awed the world with their exploits at Troy,
Prostrate under the feet of a woman.
Under the feet of two women — Aegisthus the wolf-
    bitch, tail and ears down, cowering to the pack's boss,
    Clytemnestra.
But neither sex will help him when I meet him.

CHORUS

You three Fates — hear us.
Grant us our prayers,
Let God's hand measure out
All that our hopes ask for,
As he lifts the Scales of Justice.

Justice brings everything to a balance.
For every word a word, for hatred hatred,
For every fatal stroke a fatal stroke,
For sacrilege a violent death.
For pride—the neck broken.
Three generations of suffering
Have tested the truth of this law.

ORESTES

O Father,
I am as far from you as if you
Were the centre of the earth. How
Can any words of my love,
Or loving act of my hands, reach you
Where you lie in dark nothing
For ever and ever? No breath
Of my comforting can find your cheek
To touch it. How can you hear
Our weeping eulogies,
Our hopeless laments
Through the tons of stone on your ear?
What can your blood's dust
Taste of our offerings?
How can the crushed shell of your skull know
The truth of our love?

CHORUS

Poor child, the pyre's flames that devour
The body cannot get a hold on the spirit
Of a murdered man.
His anger is merely freed.
His memory clarified and more bitter.
Then the grieving passion of his children
Crying their father's name
Is like an arrow—
Their words of mourning are barbs and feathers.
And the rites of mourning, like a bow,
Drive that arrow

Straight into the dodging heart of the killer.
The trajectory of that arrow is justice.

O Father,
Help us to bend that bow. Help us to mourn.
Look through the earth, see us,
Orestes and Electra, your children.
Let our howl
Split your tomb.
Hear your children,
Both orphaned and banished.
Rise and be with us.
Everything dies—the dust is forgotten.
How can we hope to do what has to be done?

CHORUS

Heaven can reverse evil.
Laments can turn to hymns of exultation.
The dead King's royal house, darkened with terror,
Can be lit up
By the glory-light, and the banquet torches
Of the royal ascending heir.

ORESTES

Father, you would be better
Dead beneath Troy's wall,
Slain in open battle by a brave man's weapon.
Your honour would be our wealth,
Your name our glory
In the mouths of all who remember Troy.
Your tomb, built by an army,
Towering on that coast, would be a sea-mark—
Not this heap of shame.

CHORUS

You would have shone in the underworld
Like a new star.

You would have reigned there
A King over many kings—
Just as on earth you reigned
A King over kings.

ELECTRA

Better he were not dead anywhere,
Either beside Scamander
Among those broken against the wall of Troy
Or here, tangled in a crime
That is our family's madness.
The murderers—they are the ones
Who should be dead, rotten,
And underground. Where was the accident
That could have removed both
In some casual fashion, before their plot
Snared us all in this blood-sodden knot?

CHORUS

What has happened is deaf
To the wishes of poor mortals.
Thought pleases itself—
But heaven is helpless
To change one fact.
Nevertheless, your voices combined
Make a big magic.
The powers of the earth
Are thrilled by your passion—
Also, the detested tyrant
Is crippled by his own act—
The broken law
Like a broken limb.
Soon, the voices of children,
Like an avalanche, overtake him.

ORESTES

God of the underworld,
Avenger, belated but certain—

Have we roused you
With our invocation?
From the bottom of hell
Will you come up, and take possession of us,
Out of the hidden centre
On which all turns?

Let me cry out
Over the staring corpse of Clytemnestra,
Over the gutted carcase of Aegisthus,
Let me scream
That holy scream of joy.
Why should I smother it?
If Justice shares my hope,
If God rides in the savage storm
That shakes my heart for vengeance—
Vengeance, vengeance, vengeance.

ELECTRA

I am shaking with fear.
Surely God would never let
These criminals go unpunished?
He protects the sanctity of fathers
And mothers.
Why doesn't he simply strike?
Show us the justice that is true justice.

Oh, if only you powers
Of the earth, of the night,
Of everything hidden
Would hear us.
All we ask, in all our prayers,
Is that wrong be replaced by right.

CHORUS

Be brave. Blood of the murdered
Cries from the earth for blood.

The gods have fixed that law.
The Furies, screaming for blood,
Rise like a miasma
From the fallen blood.
Pain creates pain, and ruin ruin.

ORESTES

You lords of the underworld,
You crowned and enthroned curses,
Look at us.
The last shreds of the house of Atreus—
Bereft of all but bare life,
Benighted in this darkest pit of our fate—
Lead us. Guide us.

CHORUS

When your hope falters, my heart fails.
When your courage rises, my heart leaps and rejoices.

ELECTRA

To stir up the dead
And bring them crowding the air—
Tell them the story of our mother.
She smiles and wants to stroke us.
She wants to smooth the tangles of my father's murder
    out of my hair.
The she-wolf suckles a wolf
That will rip out her throat.

CHORUS

When Agamemnon lay dead
My mourning came from the East.
I mourned him, battering my head and rending my
    breasts,
As we mourned on the dusty plains of Asia Minor.
I wrapped Agamemnon in the flowers of Troy,
And mourned them together,
Longing to die.

ELECTRA

Mother with your stone eyes, you buried him
Under a heap of stones.
No funeral, no ceremony.
A corpse rolled into a hole, and then
Instead of tears, the stones.

ORESTES

With her loveless hands she dishonoured
Not only a husband,
Not only a King—
A father
Thrown into the earth, with a laugh
Of triumph.
My hands, as pitiless as hers,
Shall draw the payment for that
From her heart.
When she is dead, my life
Will have served all its purpose.

CHORUS

Something else:
She mutilated the body of Agamemnon
As Atreus butchered
The two brothers of Aegisthus.
She made a pile, on his torso,
Of everything that could be hacked off it—
A bundled trophy, a display
To squat in your memories,
To rot your lives.

ELECTRA

What they did to his body
They did to my spirit and heart.
They flung me out
Like a dead dog
To rot in the sun.
If Agamemnon's severed head could have sobbed,

That was how I laughed.
Insane with grief.
When you want to know what grief means
Remember me.

CHORUS

CHORUS

Now let your will, like your grief,
Be stronger than life.
The past is stronger than life —
Nothing can alter it.
Now let that terrible past, like a tempered weapon,
Become your will.
Be fearless, to rip open
The future's secret.
The justice you bring
Is stronger than life.
Assume that strength.

ORESTES

Father, rise up and possess me.

ELECTRA

We are yours, Father, possess us.

CHORUS

Rise up, Agamemnon.

ORESTES

God of the sword-blade, guide my sword.
God of Judgement, decide this judgement.

ELECTRA

Gods, Gods, bring us justice.

CHORUS

The judgement deferred so long
Comes with difficulty, labour, pain —
Prayer is our only strength.

ORESTES

The demon of murder, murder on murder,
Has made our house its home—
Blood stabbing its own blood, the eyes in smoke.

ELECTRA

Bewildering sorrow, pain that stupefies.

ALL

When will it come to an end? How can it end?

ORESTES

This wound that drains our race needs a strong surgeon.
No other can prescribe
For a haemorrhage so internal.
We must find the means in ourselves.

ELECTRA

Both the blood and the wrong must be paid for in kind.

ALL

You Gods of the underworld, hear us.

CHORUS

Gods of earth, hear us.

ORESTES

Father, tipped from your throne
And slaughtered like no king,
Take your throne from your killers, bestow it on me.

ELECTRA

Father, save me from Aegisthus.

ORESTES

Then in the festivals of mourning, and in the feasts of
    remembrance, you will be honoured for ever,
Otherwise, failure for me—and for you, oblivion.

ELECTRA

Your richest festival shall be my marriage.
This tomb shall be the temple of my life.

ORESTES

O Earth, O Great Mother, direct my sword.

ELECTRA

Persephone, Queen of the Underworld,
Direct our steps.

ORESTES

Father, remember the bath where you melted to blood.

ELECTRA

Remember the cords of the net where you jerked like a
    fish.

ORESTES

Not bronze, hammered in fire,
But slender threads, woven and knotted
By a woman's fingers.

ELECTRA

Remember, trussed like a fool, and carved with laughter.

ORESTES

Surely you cannot sleep through this shame.

ELECTRA

O Father, save us, rise up, and save us.

ORESTES

Help me remove them, as they removed you.
Either by the truth of justice
Or by simple might of right.
And let me deal with them as they dealt with you.

ELECTRA

Our voice is the voice of your own race.
It lives on only through us.

ORESTES

Don't let your last seed fall into the earth, and rot.
While we live, you who are dead are alive.

ELECTRA

A man's children slip through the net of his death.
Their bodies leave his body, and bear his life
Back into life, with his name and fame.
His memories are alive in their bones.
Like the corks that buoy up the net of the fishermen
A man's children buoy up the weave of his life.
They buoy up the warp and weft of all he achieved.
Without them it sinks, lost in the depths of ocean.

ORESTES

We speak with the tongue of your death, our need is
   yours.

CHORUS

Words can do no more.
If words alone could quench it
You have more than quenched
The long thirst of this tomb.
Nothing remains but the act.
Everything waits for the act. Act
And prove that heaven and earth
Want the act done. Quickly. Now.

ORESTES

It is true, there is nothing
Left for me but to perform it.
And yet I am curious to know
What prompted the Queen to send

This troop of mourners, with wine and oil
For her husband's grave. If it be remorse,
Why so belated? Or were those
Assorted leftovers considered plenty
For such an easy victim? I think
These dregs are her latest exclamation
Of contempt, the drops of her spittle.
They say a murderer's entire wealth
Though it be the wealth of a kingdom
Cannot bribe his own conscience,
Or buy off heaven's judgement.
Why did she do it? What does it mean?

CHORUS
That I can tell you. After a nightmare
That rode her out of her sleep tearing the bedsheets,
Clutching her own mane and screaming—
She sent these gifts.

ORESTES
Did she describe this dream? Can you describe it?

CHORUS
She described it. She dreamed she was having a child.
But what came out was a big snake.

ORESTES
What else? Nothing else? Did she give it a meaning?

CHORUS
In her dream, she swaddled the snake, like a baby.
She cradled it in her arms, and she kissed it.

ORESTES
How did she feed this child that was no child?

CHORUS
She pushed her nipple into the fanged jaws.

ORESTES

Surely—the fangs sank into her breast.

CHORUS

Yes, and blood came out with the milk. The snake
Chewed on milk and blood curdling together.

ORESTES

She was right. This dream crept from her husband's
grave.

CHORUS

She woke screaming, clawing the wall of her
bedchamber.
Torches were lit up throughout the palace
Till the place blazed with light, and she sat sobbing,
Suddenly terrified of Agamemnon.

ORESTES

One more prayer—to the earth that embraces my
father's bones.
Let me be the meaning of this nightmare.
Let my sword interpret it. This reptile
Emerged as I did, out of her belly.
It was wrapped by her, as I was wrapped,
In baby cloths. Its mouth was plugged
As mine was plugged, by her oozing nipple,
And the snake sucked her milk, as I did.
But if its mouth, its trap of fangs,
Bit into her breast, and gulped blood
Out of her heart, and brought her screaming
To break through the wall of her bedchamber—
The meaning is plain. I am that snake.
I shall not kiss my mother. When I strike
Every drop of blood in her body
Will make a single coagulated lump
The shape of Clytemnestra.
And when she hits the wall

That screaming mouth will stiffen in its mask.
Her dream is our fate—hers and mine.
She must die and I must murder her.

CHORUS
Your logic has the temper of bronze.
You know your friends; tell us:
Which of us must do what? A clear plan.

ORESTES
Electra, you go back into the palace.
Your part is to allay any suspicion.
Treachery gave them the throne, and treachery
Will take it from them, at the same price:
Then the prophecy of Apollo's priest
Will be perfect, as it always has been perfect.

Here is my part:
I shall arrive at the gate of the palace
With Pylades. The guards there
Will see two foreigners
Dressed like men from Phocis,
Speaking in the accents of Phocis—
And announcing that they have come to the palace
With a purpose. Then if the guards
Tell us we've picked a bad moment
And that the house is closed
Because of some supernatural event,
Then we'll wait right there at the gate
Till folk in the street cry out: 'Shame on Aegisthus,
Keeping his gate shut against travellers.'
However it goes,
Once I get inside the palace
And see that creature Aegisthus
Squatting on my father's throne
Or meet him face to face,
That moment is his last.

Before he can say 'What is your name?'
My blade will split his heart.
This house has been the goblet
That the demon of homicide, unquenchable,
Has loved to drain.
Today let it swallow its third
And last fill of the blood
That has poisoned us all.

Electra, keep watch for us
Inside the palace.
Let nobody spring
Our simple trap.
You women, say nothing. Or speak only
As if you knew nothing.

And you, Hermes,
God of the dark pathways, guide my sword.
Make it the royal road to the underworld
For these killers.

CHORUS

The earth implants,
In everything born, a terror.
Ocean is a slow, cold eruption
Of devourers, devouring each other.
And all hide from the sun's flaming gape
That will consume this globe.
Hurricanes come over the horizon
And out of man's heart,
Out of his pride and out of his furious will.
And out of woman's womb
Comes the tornado
That spins its double face of love and hatred
In the giddy passion
That flings marriage off, like a garment,
And shames the animals.

Remember Althaea.
A log burning in the hearth
Held the entire life of the boy that moment
Sliding from her belly—Meleager.
She snatched that glowing log up and she dowsed it
And locked it away, and kept it unconsumed,
Cherished it as she cherished Meleager.
Till he was man enough
To murder her two brothers in a quarrel
About a beautiful woman and a dead pig.
Althaea's scream of fury was twisted
With the death-screams of her son
As she burned that log to ashes—

Another woman, worse—
Scylla.
The daughter of Nisus, King of Megara.
When Minos, the King of Crete,
Besieged Megara
Nisus butchered his warriors
With impunity.
Under the city walls, day after day,
Nisus roamed the battlefield
Invulnerable
So long as a single purple curl of hair
That sprang from his fontanelle
Nested in the white mane, under his helmet.
Minos, from his tent,
Promised Scylla his love.
He bribed her with a golden torque
To sharpen a razor
And bring him the purple tress
From the head of her sleeping father.
His promised love was her madness.
Scylla threw her father to the hyena,
Helpless and unprotected
As any common man,
For an embrace that would destroy her.

The gods detest these women.
Our whole sex is dishonoured
By these women.
No man will honour
What the gods find detestable.

The sword is poised
Close to the heart.
Justice drives it home.
None can ignore
The laws of heaven
That stand between right and wrong.

Justice is the anvil where Fate
Forges the blade.
Murder begets murder.
A life must pay for a life.
The avenger,
The demon of patience and cunning,
Waits for the moment,
Then demands the full price.

(Orestes knocks at palace gate.)

SERVANT

Who's there? Who's there?

ORESTES

Strangers at the gate!
Travellers at the gate!
If the house of Aegisthus
With open door
Honours custom—
We are strangers, with news.

SERVANT

Enough! Enough!
You'll wake the dead.

Where are you from?
What are your names?

ORESTES

Tell your master two strangers stand at the gate
With news he wants to know, news from far off.
And hurry. We arrive almost too late,
In the last glow of the West.
Soon even the friendliest inn
Will be shutting its doors against travellers.
My news needs to be heard by the master of the house,
Unless a woman rules.
In that case, she should hear it.
But a man would be better —
Then I can be blunt
And go straight to the point.
Also, my evidence is of a kind
I would prefer to reveal first to a man.

(Enter Clytemnestra.)

CLYTEMNESTRA

If your news is so important, let me have it.
The open hospitality of this house
Is famed throughout Argos.
Everything is yours — hot baths, cool beds,
With a welcome fitted to your station,
And every entertainment. What is this news?

ORESTES

I come from Phocis, I am a merchant —
Brought here by the market of Argos.
But your gate is my first stop.
On my way here I met a man,
Strophius, also from Phocis —
A stranger to me up to that moment.
When he heard of my destination
He asked if I would like to carry some news

To the King of Argos.
'It might do you some good,' he told me.
'This is the news, remember it:
Orestes is dead.
Deliver this message,' he said,
'And tell them he has been burned according to
    custom,
With all the ceremonies necessary,
And that his ashes lie in a bronze casket.
Tell them this. His family can decide
Whether to carry his ashes home
And bury them in the tomb of his father,
Or to leave them in Phocis,
Where the earth will treat him no less kindly.'
This is my news. Perhaps I am speaking to one
Who understands what I am saying.
Perhaps my words mean more than I know.

CLYTEMNESTRA

Aaah!
The curse on the blood of this house
Has tracked down the last drop.
Nobody can escape you.
Our last hope drained, and our life shattered like a
    goblet.
I hide my treasures away
But you sniff them out,
And scatter them in air, and leave me bereft.
Orestes was prudent.
Prudent, far-seeing, circumspect—
Only he
Remained unstained to reverse the curse.
He kept his foot out of this quag
That sucks to the centre of the earth.
But only for a few summers of illusion—
Now the Fury
Writes his name
In his own ashes.

ORESTES

Forgive me.
It would have been far better for me too
If I had brought good news
To a house of such high fortune, such splendour.
Then I could have tasted the bounty
Of your royal hospitality untainted.
But I bound myself
To deliver the news
You needed to know—
Sharp as it is.
Not to have come to your gate with what I have to give
    you
Would have been wrong.
And you have received me with much understanding.

CLYTEMNESTRA

You have earned all you could hope for.
Stranger, this house is your house,
With every comfort you need.
Some other would have brought what you have
    brought.
Men who have come from far off, as you have,
And still have far to go, as you have,
Need what we shall give you tonight.
Show them their chambers.
See everything done for them as for my own family.
Aegisthus shall hear this news.
Our councillors
Will help us decide what to make of it.

(She goes in.)

CHORUS

Women are physically weak.
But the strongest man, and the most violent,
Is weaker than his mother.
Now is the time to give our strength to Orestes.

You heap of earth
Covering Agamemnon —
Like the load of grief
That oppresses those who mourn him,
Hear our prayer.
Breathe power into the cunning of Orestes.
Put a new edge on his sword.
Guide it through the lightning split second
That determines a life.

(Enter Cilissa.)

Our man from Phocis is making himself felt.
This is Cilissa, once the nurse of Orestes.
Cilissa, what have you heard? What has happened?

CILISSA

The Queen wanted Aegisthus
To hear the news from the strangers.
She has sent me to bring him.
Now she has heard the news herself
Her face is a mask of grief.
She wears it for us — but through that mask
Her eyes blaze with joy.
Her wild sobbing
Is a kind of uncontrollable laughter.
This news, which is the death-blow
To the lineage of Agamemnon,
For her is harvest home.
Hearing this, Aegisthus
Will also weep — yes, weep for joy.
He will collapse in his chair
And bury his face, he will hide his face in his hands
Incredulous with joy.
Aah!
In the reign of Atreus
Horror after horror, grief after grief,
Dragged every nerve from my body.

I thought I had done with feeling.
I thought I could bear anything
Like a stone in the flow.
But now— Oh, Orestes,
Orestes is dead! Orestes!
I took him fresh from his mother's womb,
Fragrant as an armful of flowers.
It was my milk he drank,
Like a blind kitten.
It was me he cried for.
Night after night, it was me
He wore out with endless wants.
Through whole nights I held him,
Rocking his sleeping trust in my arms—
He was my life.
And I was his life.
A baby is helpless at both ends.
I understood the dumb cries
Of his two needs.
And as he grew up, I was his wisdom.
It was me he came to.
His father away in Troy—
I was the oracle for Orestes.
I was the very voice of the earth itself
For Orestes.
And now I must bring this man
Who is hardly a man,
The murderer of Agamemnon,
To hear the best news of his life—
That Orestes is dead.

CHORUS

How is Aegisthus to present himself
To these strangers? Are there any instructions?

CILISSA

Should he come with his bodyguard?
Aegisthus never stirs without bodyguard.

No. Tell him to come alone.
Tell him these men are timid merchants
Who will be too easily overawed —
Too easily scared into silence.
Urge him to put them at their ease.
If he wants the whole story, tell him
He must come alone.

CILISSA

Are you so anxious for the whole story to be told
Of the death of Orestes? The death of our last hope?

CHORUS

What if the great hand of Zeus
Should change the story, like a wind,
To blow in the opposite direction?

CILISSA

How can it change? Orestes, our hope, is dead.

CHORUS

Prophets cannot be sure of anything.

CILISSA

Is there other news? What have you heard?

CHORUS

Go and deliver your message. Bring Aegisthus
To hear the biggest news he ever will hear.
And leave the work of the gods — to the gods.

(Nurse goes.)

Zeus, you God over all gods,
All that we pray for is justice.
Let the misfortunes of this house
Be corrected — according to justice.

Let all who have prayed for justice
See the throne of Argos today
Return to the rule of justice.

The son of Agamemnon
Stands in his own palace.
Now bring the detestable one,
As a beast, to be sacrificed
To justice.

Zeus, you loved Agamemnon.
Make the way clear for his son
To reach the murderer
With the sword of your justice.

You Gods of the house,
Lift the judgement that has kept it dark.
Wash the signature of blood
Off the deeds
That gave this house to the curse.
Lord of the deep cavern, Apollo,
Let this house
Be raised from the grave
Now
By its rightful master
With a single movement
Of his right arm.

Hermes, son of Maia,
Rise and stand at the shoulder of Orestes
Like a wind filling a sail.
Let the breath of your cunning
Prompt the tongue of Orestes
To fling the net of words over the tyrant
And liberate Argos.

Be strong, Orestes.
When you drive your sword into your mother

Deafen yourself
With the death-cry of Agamemnon.
When she wails 'Orestes, my child'
Deafen yourself to her voice
And shout: 'I belong to my murdered father.'
Kill her, and be done with it.
Your sword is the tool of Fate.
You cannot be blamed.
Harden yourself, Orestes,
Like the polished shield
That reflected the face of the Gorgon.
Do it for those who depend on you
For justice,
For the living and the dead who depend on you.
Do it for the house of Atreus.
With one twist of that blade
Dig out the root of the curse—
Cut through the tap root of the vendetta
That opens deadly flowers at our doors and windows.
Split the source of the seed
With your blade.

(Enter Aegisthus.)

AEGISTHUS
Where are these merchants with their shocking news
Of the death of Orestes?
It may be no more than a rumour,
But uncertainty is painful.
This is an evil day, if they bring truth.
Are we to think the curse on this house
Is delivering its latest—
On top of what is already intolerable?
Every new cry of alarm makes the heart shake with
    dread.
Is this the truth?
Or is it a shock wave of hysteria
From a panic among women,

A panic that flares up and burns out
Like a handful of straw?
What am I to think?

We heard this news.
But our grief
Will distort it
Even as we tell it.
The merchants are waiting:
Ask them for the truth—
Simple and plain.

Where are they? Let me hear them.
Let me hear what is known
From those who know it.
And the first question first: 'Were you there when he
    died?
Or is this one more rumour
Picked up in some market place?'
Better for them if they give me the hard fact.
They're dealing with a man who sees through men and
    the mesh of words.

(Aegisthus goes in.)

CHORUS

Zeus, Zeus—
Dumb
We pray.
No words
For the prayer
To guide this moment,
To level the blade,
To set the point
And slam the hilt
To the ribcage.

This day's end
Will bring us either
The end of this house
Of Agamemnon
Or justice.
Now it is the turn
Of Orestes
To act for Fate.
To grip his sword
With the hand of God.

(Death-cry of Aegisthus.)

CHORUS

Which voice was that? Whose death-cry was that?
Who is our master now?
Say nothing, do nothing, till we know.
Either the best has happened, or the worst.
Our lives have been decided.

(Enter Servant.)

SERVANT

Aegisthus is dead!
Aegisthus is dead!
Where are the bodyguards?
Is everybody deaf?
Aegisthus has been murdered.
Where is the Queen?
Warn Clytemnestra.
With terrible strength
A maniac
Has disembowelled Aegisthus
And torn out his heart.
Warn the Queen
To protect herself—

(Enter Clytemnestra.)

CLYTEMNESTRA

What is all the yelling about?
Are you out of your minds? This is a palace—

SERVANT

The dead have risen, they butcher the living.

CLYTEMNESTRA

I knew it! Ah! I knew it!
I could not believe it possible but I knew it.
By cunning we killed—now cunning will kill us.
Bring me a weapon. O God, let it be settled.
Let this long, bloody coil
Come at last
To the final twist.

(Enter Orestes.)

ORESTES

He has paid the price. Now it is your turn.

CLYTEMNESTRA

Oh, my love! Couldn't that huge strength help you?

ORESTES

Since he was your love you shall sleep with him.
Dead, you will never be false to a dead man.

CLYTEMNESTRA

Orestes, my child! Don't point at me with your sword.
See these breasts that fed you when you were helpless.
These were your first pillows when you were helpless.

(Enter Pylades.)

ORESTES

Pylades, can a man kill his mother?
Can he perform anything more dreadful

Than the murder of his own mother?
What shall I do?

PYLADES

Remember the words of Apollo.
Obey the command of the god of the oracle.
Embrace the enmity of mankind
Rather than be false to the word of heaven.

ORESTES

Wise words, and spoken at the right moment.
Go in.
Mother, I am going to kill you now,
On the corpse of your darling.
When both were alive, you preferred him to my father.
Now both are dead, you are stuck with your bargain for
    ever.

CLYTEMNESTRA

I gave you your life, Orestes. Let me have mine.

ORESTES

Here in this house, where you stole the life of my
    father.

CLYTEMNESTRA

Do not blame me. I was in the hand of Fate.

ORESTES

And now the same hand holds this sword.

CLYTEMNESTRA

Oh, my son, remember the curse of a parent.

ORESTES

Yes, you gave me life,
Then made sure it was wretched.
A life

Of misery, bitterness, humiliation—
And the worse that is still to come.
After I have killed you. This was your gift:
You gave me life, then spat me out as a curse.

CLYTEMNESTRA
I tried to protect you. Our trusted friends
Were your guardians: I arranged it.

ORESTES
I was born heir to the throne—you bartered us away—
Both me and my throne.

CLYTEMNESTRA
How did I barter you?
You are talking like a madman. What was your price?

ORESTES
That carcase. I shame to name or describe it.

CLYTEMNESTRA
Your father was not so faithful—are you forgetting?

ORESTES
He laboured in battle while you—played on his bed.

CLYTEMNESTRA
A woman without her man learns desperation.

ORESTES
A woman owes her place and her safety to her man.

CLYTEMNESTRA
Will you murder your own mother?

ORESTES
Me murder you?
Mother, you have already murdered yourself.
I merely hold the sword as you fall.

CLYTEMNESTRA

Remember the Furies that rise from the blood of a
   mother.

ORESTES

If I relent, who lives with my father's curse?

CLYTEMNESTRA

This is my dream! Here is the snake
That crawled out of my womb and bit my breasts.

ORESTES

Your dream was no dream but prophecy.
Your crime was sacrilege.
Your punishment shall be sacrilege, the same.

(Orestes drives in Clytemnestra.)

CHORUS

A two-headed monster of guilt—
But we must mourn them.
Our prince has put a crown of blood
On the terrible past
At his own cost
But at least he has given life to the hope of Argos.

Judgement was slow
To catch up with the thief who came from Troy.
But in the end his city had to pay.
His entire people paid.
Judgement was slow, also,
To disentangle Aegisthus
From the limbs of Clytemnestra—
Slow, but sure.

Shout for joy! Shout!

The arms that wielded the treacherous sword
Have attracted the counterstroke

Of lightning from heaven.
And the two stricken corpses
Make a new monument of Justice.

Shout for joy! Shout!

Apollo, god of the deep cave
Beneath Parnassus,
Spoke his riddle:
'Wrap my word of truth in an act of falsehood.'
Justice
Justifies Apollo.
The designs of heaven
Weave man into the pattern.
His agony must submit
To the omnipotent
In patience.

Shout for joy! Shout!

Time has come full term—
Justice, newly delivered
As a full-grown prince,
Will step out through these doors,
Opening the palace to the light,
Cleansing the hearth of blood,
Washing the curse
From the walls and floors and ceilings
Where it has thickened so long.
All who speak of this house
Shall tell of its new blessings—
Fortune's own palace.

(Corpses revealed.)

ORESTES

Here are the tyrants.
These are my father's murderers.

The murderers of your King, Agamemnon.
And all that was bequeathed to me by my father
These two plundered.
When they were alive, they shared
One throne, one bed and the whole wealth of Argos.
Now they are dead—they share only death.
They swore an oath—to trap my father
And to butcher him in his helplessness.
They swore another oath—to live together
And to die together. How happy they are!
All their oaths are fulfilled.

You who will judge me—look at this.
This is the subtle apparatus
That transformed my father
From the conqueror of Troy—to a helpless fish.
It bound him and trussed him up in a thousand knots.
Display it. Let everybody see it.
Let every man imagine himself
Bound and wound within it.
Imagine the tormentors
Laughing as the sword goes in, through the meshes.
Look at it. Let the Father look at it—
Not my father—the Father of All
Who sees everything on earth.
Let him see this work of my mother's.
Let the sun look at it and be sickened.
I want his word
That all I did was according to right.
I shall need his witness
When I am tried for murdering my mother.

I bear no guilt for killing Aegisthus.
On him I merely exacted the law
That condemns adulterers.
But what about her
Who wove this web
And plotted the murder

Of the man whose only son
Was her only son, her best-loved child,
Though now he has killed her?
What about her?
She is so venomous,
Crammed so full of malignant evil
If she were a viper she would need no fangs.
She would kill at a touch—
One caress and her victim
Would be bloating, like a corpse in the sun,
A gangrenous horror.
What is this contraption of hers?
A snare for a dangerous animal
Or the winding-cloths of a dead man?
Some perverse bandit
Might have designed it, to drop over travellers
And make his killing easy,
Stuffing the guilt away beneath his laughter.
God keep my house from such a woman—
Better to die childless.

CHORUS

We must mourn the King you killed,
And weep for your triumph.
His death was hard.
But wrong has a root,
And this is its flower.

ORESTES

Is she guilty? Or is she innocent?
See this bloodied cloak, see the rips in it—
You recognise the cloak of Agamemnon?
This is the work of Aegisthus. Here and here.
It is also my witness.
Look where the blood has dried
And decayed in the figured cloth.
I praise my father, after too long a silence.

And since I never saw his dead body
I lament over what killed him—
This loathsome coil of meshes.

What my mother did is my torment.
Now her punishment is my torment.
And my triumph
Has made what is left of my life
A torment.

CHORUS

Who escapes pain and trouble?
Who escapes ,
From beginning to end, happy?
Sorrows either are here now
Or are coming.
Time and the gods unfailingly bring them.

ORESTES

I am like a man in a chariot
Losing control
Of the horses,
Plunging towards I do not know what.
I am hanging on to the reins
Without the strength
To do more than merely hang on,
My brain in a whirl,
My heart crouching in terror.

While I am still sane and among you
Let me declare this—
You who are loyal will understand me:
It was not a sin to kill my mother.
From head to foot, she was polluted
With my father's blood.
The gods detested her.
Apollo gave me the strength

To perform this act of justice.
The great god commanded me to do it.
His oracle made it clear:
If I killed my mother I would not be guilty.
And if I did not kill her—
My punishment cannot be told.
Mind cannot bear to imagine it.

Watch me now. Protected by these leaves,
I am going to the temple of the centre of the earth—
Apollo's house
Where the everlasting flame
Burns for the god.
That place is my sanctuary.
Apollo told me
To flee there and be safe
After I had punished my mother.
Let all men of Argos, now and in the future,
Witness my innocence.
My mother's death was decided
In heaven
By the gods.
I was simply their weeping instrument.
Remember this, report what I had to do
In these words. And tell how I left this place
A fugitive and an exile.

CHORUS

You are Justice itself.
You have enacted Justice.
Don't foul the fact, in all its brilliance,
With such gloomy words.
Have the courage of your destiny.
You have liberated Argos, your own land.
The two monsters that held this land in terror
You have killed.
You should be shouting for joy.

ORESTES

Ah!
Look there—look: women, in grey cloaks,
With the faces of Gorgons. Don't you see them?
Their bodies and their heads wreathed with vipers—
They are coming.

CHORUS

Our prince, Orestes, the most loyal son
A father ever had—
This is your day of triumph.
All your enemies are dead.
All Argos rejoices in you.
These are hallucinations
After your inhuman exertions
Defeating the greatest of all human terrors.
You have nothing to fear.

ORESTES

These women are real—spirits have power
Over the spirit of a man.
That is not imagination.
These demons are the decomposition
Of my mother's blood.
They are the wolves of her body, of her breasts, of her
    womb.

CHORUS

You are confused. Your innocence
Horrifies itself—it sees goblins
When you look at the blood on your hands.
That is natural. Therefore we have a ritual
To wash your hands clean.

ORESTES

Apollo! The earth is teeming
With these creatures—

Apollo, you did not warn me!
They are climbing out of the earth,
Out of their burrows in old blood.
Eyes like weeping ulcers,
Mouths like fetid wounds.
Their whips whistle and crack.

CHORUS

Hurry to Apollo's temple —
Apollo will cleanse you.
Apollo will wash your eyes clear of these visions.

ORESTES

You cannot see them but I see them.
You cannot feel their whips but I feel them.
Aaah!

(Exit Orestes.)

CHORUS

Only God can help Orestes.
May God help him.
May God guide his blind steps finally
To peace.

You see how the ancient curse on this house
Strikes for the third time, like a thunderbolt.
And how the terrible blood splashes at last
Into the hands of a good and innocent man.
The butchery of Thyestes' children began it.
Next came the treachery of Clytemnestra,
Who stabbed her royal husband, Agamemnon,
As he stripped to wash off the blood of his enemies.
A madness began it, brother against brother.
Madness redoubled it, wife against husband.
Is this third the last — son against mother?
How can Orestes break the ring of madness?

Can the poor, scorched brains of Orestes
Figure out all the factors? Can he solve
The arithmetic of the unfinished
That shunts this curse from one generation to the next?
Who can bring it to an end?
When can it be brought to an end?
How can it be brought to an end?

THE EUMENIDES

(At Apollo's temple.)

PRIESTESS

In my prayers, first
I pray to Earth—mother of prophecy.
Then to Themis—Earth's titanic daughter,
Whose oracle this was.
Then to Phoebe—also daughter of Earth.
She succeeded to this oracular throne,
Then gave it as a gift
To Phoebus. Phoebus Apollo.
His accession
Was a procession long as the land is wide.
It trampled the pilgrim road through virgin forest.
Apollo, honoured by the King and the people.
Son of God. And God gave Apollo
The mind and the tongue
To speak the truth of God to mankind.
To open the future, to unriddle the present,
Where mankind huddles blindly, at a shut door.
These come first in my prayer.
Next comes Athene,
And the nymphs of the cave
Of Dionysus,
Who possessed the Bassarids, his women,
To hunt King Pentheus and rip him to pieces,
As hounds hunt a hare and rip it to pieces.
Next comes the river of Delphi.
Next Poseidon, whose ocean embraces the earth.
Last, Zeus, Father of All.

Now I take my seat
In the breath of the god.
Only let today
Bring blessings greater than any day yet.

Those Greeks who have come to ask
The oracle a question:

Let them draw lots.
As Apollo breathes through me, I shall speak.

(Priestess goes in to shrine. She staggers out again, with shrieks.)

A horrible vision! No, it wasn't a vision.
I can hardly stand.
Hold me up. It wasn't a vision.
Oh, too much for an old woman—
I'm weaker than a baby.
I went in,
Towards the shrine.
The inner shrine is hung with the wreaths of suppliants.
It is centred on the stone of the earth's centre.
The omphalos. The holiest of all stones.
On that stone a strange man is sitting.
A man dipped in blood,
His whole body varnished with blood,
And he grips a sword, also bloody,
As though his grip had locked on the hilt
And he could not relax it.
His eyes stare, as if he could not blink
Or dare not blink.
Yet he knows where he is—
Fresh olive leaves,
With white new wool twisted among them,
Are bound around his head,
Acknowledging Apollo.
His appearance is terrifying.
But worse—I cannot describe it—
Around him, on the stone benches,
Strange sleeping creatures.
I would call them women but they are not women.
Gorgon-faced—yet not Gorgons.
Black, like the rags of soot that hang in a chimney,
Like bats, yet wingless.
Each of their faces a mess of weeping ulcers—

The eyes, the mouth, ulcers.
Their bodies exhale
A stench like maggoty corpses.
Their cloaks are saturated and stained
With their own putrescence
That oozes from them, into the stones.
Who are they? What are they?
Some other kind—inhuman.
Monsters from a different world
To be cursed by God and men.
Apollo is powerful.
And this is his temple.
All human pollutions
Await his cleansing touch.
Priest, prophet, healer—
I leave this stranger to him.

(She goes. Enter Apollo and Orestes.)

APOLLO

Orestes, I am beside you.
Wherever you range
I guard your steps
And disable your enemies.
The Furies are quiet.
These hags, from outside time,
From inside space, whose emergence
Appals God and man and beast,
Born in evil, living in their unlit
Underworld of evil,
Hated by gods and men—
For a while they sleep. Now is your chance.
Hurry. Be off. Be strong.
They will hunt you through the mountains,
And over the continent,
They will hunt you from island to island,
City to city.
Wherever earth can be trodden, they will pursue you.

Do not weaken.
Do not jettison
Your allotted suffering—
Bear it as a wealth
To Athens, the city of Athene.
There, embrace the image of Athene—
Beg for her help.
Lay your suffering down at her feet.

There you shall be judged
By men that I have appointed.
And there, inspiring the tongue,
I will free you.
I commanded you to murder your mother.
Now I shall draw, as in a lottery,
From all your tossed-up days and nights,
Deliverance from the crime.

ORESTES

Apollo—of all gods you are the god
Of justice.
I commit my whole life
To your guidance
And your promise.

APOLLO

Above all—keep your courage.
Firm as the blade
That never wavered
When it did the work.

Hermes, my brother,
Guide him. Guard him.
This outlaw is holy
In the eyes of God.

(All go. Enter the Ghost of Clytemnestra.)

CLYTEMNESTRA'S GHOST

Wake up! Wake up! Wake up!
You are forgetting me.
You are neglecting my cause.
The dead begin to remember
The man I killed and they curse me.
They drive me through the underworld,
Screaming after me: 'There she goes,
The murderess of Agamemnon!
That's her! The monster Clytemnestra!'
I stumble and run ashamed, contemptible
To all the hordes of hell.
They accuse me, charge me, try me, convict me
As if my son had never touched me.
Wake up. Get to work!
Let the worlds know why you are hunting Orestes—
Raise the cry.
Look at this wound he made, here under my ribs
When the sword point came out at the back of my
    neck.
That was my son's homecoming gift.
Daylight makes a wall of the flesh,
But sleep can see through the earth.
Remember the midnights
I conjured you—
With libations and the burning of banquets.

It was all a waste.
He has leapt out of the trap
Like a hare from a clump of grass—
Gone, laughing at you
While you snore and slumber on.
You powers of the earth, hear me.
Hear me in your sleep—
Clytemnestra was murdered by her own son.
Clytemnestra!
She is screaming to you from under the earth.

(Chorus of Furies stirs.)

You stir—but your prey flies.
He has better allies. His
Help him at every corner—but mine sleep.

(Chorus stirs.)

Wake up! Death is too ready to take you back
Into his shiftlessness. Have you forgotten
Orestes who murdered his mother?
He's getting away! He's gone.

(Chorus more agitated.)

Sleep and exhaustion together
Are too much even for these horrors.

CHORUS

After him! Catch him! Seize him!
Catch him! Catch him! Catch him!
After him! After him!

CLYTEMNESTRA

You hunt in your sleep, like dogs,
But what about your duty?
Can sleep overpower the Furies?
Have you forgotten my pain?
Strip his conscience naked
With your whips of words dipped in acid.
Deafen him
With blasts of outrage and execration
From your wombs.
Paralyse the brain in his skull
With despair.
Hunt him into his grave.

(Chorus wakes up.)

FURIES

Awake! Awake! Awake!
What was that voice?
What has happened?
Orestes has tricked us.
We have overslept
Like simple fools—
Our duty went off
In a dream!
Look, the blood on that stone.
There our prey fed and rested
While we slept.
Apollo, you are a god
But you behave like a trickster.
You ignore the old rules.
You contradict and defy
The older powers.
You call it justice
To convince a man that his mother
Must be executed,
Then protect the matricide—
As if motherhood
Were some accident—
Better forgotten.
How can that be justice? How can it be right?

You have forgotten, you god of the bright day,
The voice of sleep.
The voice that pierces me
And jabs me awake
Like the goad in the buttock of the ox
As it staggers at the plough.
Remorse. You have forgotten
The blind fury out of pitch darkness—
Remorse.
A voice out of the belly of Fate itself.
The silent unending scream that brings a man down.

It is not our fault.
Blame the new gods
Who buried the older powers
Under the floors of their own shrines
And ruled from new altars—
Altars drenched with blood.
Look at that stone—
The most sacred seat of the older powers,
The powers who once owned this temple—
See what you have done to it.

Apollo, you may be the god of prophets,
You may be the wisest of gods—
But you have broken the laws—
The oldest laws that destiny
Wove into the brains and bodies of men.
You have rejected their claim—and you have done it
To help one man.

You are the enemy of Fate.
And you are mine too.
You shall not protect
Such a criminal,
The murderer of his mother.
A curse, inescapable and heavy,
Has locked onto the head of Orestes,
And wherever he goes, it goes.
His head is the iron cage
Of that curse.
Wherever he stands, or sits, his eyes
Peer out through those bars.
He is held in that cage, his own prisoner,
Till an avenger comes—
One of his own kind, the equaliser,
With the key in his hand—
The sleepless sword of the house of Atreus.

(Enter Apollo.)

APOLLO

Get out of this temple—all of you.
This place is sacred to prophecy.
Get out—you know my arrows,
My flame-headed darts
That will boil your entrails
And bring out of your mouths the reeking lumps
Of what you have gulped from corpses.
You do not belong here—
These walls are defiled by your presence.
You belong in the dungeon
Furnished for torturers,
The den of castration, mutilation,
Flaying, dismemberment, impalement—
That is your banqueting hall.
Where eyes are extracted, windpipes drawn,
Livers and bowels shaken onto the floor,
Heads twisted from shoulders—
That is your study.
The chamber of screams is your rest-place.
For which you are detested by heaven.
Look at you:
From the talons of your feet
To the deadly snakes that crown you
Everything about you
Witnesses the truth of what I have said.
Get out.
Find the slaughter-midden of some lion
And sleep among the putrid bones—
Take your living corpses
Out of this blessed precinct.
Out. Out. Out.

CHORUS

Now I speak.
You, Apollo, are to blame
For everything that Orestes has done.
Orestes obeyed you—

But you obeyed no one.
It was your oracle
Commanded him to kill his mother
And guaranteed him immunity for a crime
That was agony to the earth.

APOLLO

My oracle
Ordered him to avenge his father.

CHORUS

Bloodied by her blood
He ran to you for protection.

APOLLO

I told him
To flee to the safety of the temple.

CHORUS

We are his sacred escort. Why
Do you revile us?

APOLLO

You desecrate this temple.

CHORUS

Our presence here, with Orestes,
Is our duty.
We are our duty.

APOLLO

A glorious duty! A noble duty!

CHORUS

A duty imposed on us by the earth—
To harry the matricide, to hunt him
Out of his land, and out of his wits.

APOLLO

When a wife murders her husband, who hunts her?

CHORUS

Wife and husband share no lineal blood.
Whatever her act may be called
It is not sacrilege.

APOLLO

So breaking the holy contract of marriage
Blessed and sealed by Zeus and Hera,
Breaking it
In a violent passion, with a murderous weapon,
Is not sacrilege?
Rolling the corpse of the bridegroom
Into the lap of the Queen of Heaven and Earth,
Great Aphrodite,
Who blesses man with his greatest happiness—
That is not sacrilege?

The most sacred agreement, more sacred
That any blind eruption of pain
Out of the earth,
The most sacred agreement among men
Is the marriage contract
Which binds two total strangers to love each other,
To protect each other
And blend their love in a third, who loves both.

But you recognise no contract
With the father,
Neither between his wife and him
Nor between him and his son, whose blood he shares.
The earth is like a mad elephant
When a son murders his mother.
But the same earth is deaf
When father is murdered by mother,

And deaf again when the son avenges his father.
This may be the law of the earth
But it is not human justice.
Only Athene, great Goddess of Wisdom,
Can judge this. She shall hear our call.

CHORUS

I shall never leave Orestes.

APOLLO

After him, then. Do your worst.

CHORUS

Apollo, not even your words shall limit our licence.

APOLLO

I would not take your licence as a gift.

CHORUS

You may be important in heaven,
One of the greatest in the circle of the gods,
But I shall sniff out Orestes
By the smell of his mother's blood.
I shall bring him to bay
And I shall demand justice.

APOLLO

Orestes asked me for help.
In hell, on earth, and in heaven I shall help him.
You tell of the earth's anger.
But this is my duty—to stand by Orestes.
And should I ever forsake him
Hell and earth and heaven would crumble
Into a chaos
Of rage against me.

(*Temple of Athene. Enter Orestes.*)

Divine Athene! Hear me!
Apollo directed me to your temple
Here in Athens.
Be patient with me, Athene.
Hear my story to the end.
Favour me with your judgement.
I am a fugitive
But no longer polluted.
The dust of many towns, many cities,
Has scoured the blood from my fingers.
Their stones have blunted my guilt.
A thousand welcoming doorways
Have washed the filth of my crime from my feet.
I have worn out the Furies
In the tangle of earth's roads,
In the maze of tracks and pathways.
And at last I have reached your temple.
Obedient to Apollo
Here I stand in front of your effigy
Surrendering my trial, my hope, my life
To your judgement!
And here I shall stay till you have judged me.

(Enter Chorus of Furies.)

CHORUS

His trail glows clear—like a track of fire.
Invisible and silent—the spoor
Of the polluted man.
The smell of his mother's womb clings to his heels
And sweats from his instep.
Plain as the blood-splashed route of a wounded stag
In the noses of the hounds.

Again and again he has tricked us and escaped us.
Again and again, in every corner

Of every land, we have sniffed him out.
He cannot escape us for long.
We have skimmed over seas, wingless,
And bounded among high peaks,
Running him down. Again and again
We have found him, sleeping exhausted.
We have collapsed around him, exhausted,
And again he has slipped away, and always escaped us.

Now he is here. Where is he?
He has squeezed himself into some cranny
Like a bat. He is here, somewhere.
The reek of his fear is thick in the air.

Look! There! That's him.
The matricide.
Block the door, close the trap,
Don't let him get away.
Once again he's found a refuge
From the taste of our whips—this time
Clinging to the statue of a goddess
And begging for a justice
Kinder than these lashes
That slice at his heart and flay his spirit.
There is no hope for Orestes.
His mother's blood, with the voice of earth,
Convicts him from the earth—
He can never compel it
To go back into her body.
Now you shall pay us, Orestes,
For the blood of your mother
With your own, which was hers.
Your guilty soul
Shall render to us
The rags of the body
She gave you.
As long as you live
Your body will render

To us these dues.
Fate has granted
Your body to us—
To hunt, and consume,
Till you are dead.

Nobody alive
Can escape
The exact accounting
For sin against heaven,
Sin against parent, sin against guest,
Payment of flesh—payment
In the suffering of the body.
Flesh is the food
Of the earth's justice.

Death sits in session
Over man's days.
None can escape
The register
Of his every word, his every thought
Kept by death.

ORESTES

Pain has taught me much and it has taught me
The wisdom of rituals.
I know when I have licence to speak
And when to be silent.
Now I am commanded to speak
By a wise prompter.
The blood has been washed from my hands.

I have cleansed myself
Of the guilt of matricide
With the blood-offerings at the shrine of Apollo.
Many have given me hospitality
Without being polluted by my presence.
Now I call on the city of Athens,

With holy words
I call on the great goddess Athene
Whose wisdom rules Athens.
I call on her to help me.
Myself, my own land of Argos,
And all who belong to Argos
Shall be hers, bound to her
In a sacred alliance,
If she will help me.
Wherever she roams,
Wherever she declares her presence
In the deathless courage and good fortune
Of her worshippers, and in the unconquerable
Spirit of her armies,
I call on her
To judge my case, and to save me.

CHORUS

Apollo cannot save you.
Athene cannot save you.
Outcast, banished from all joy,
You can only live now.
As a spectre, possessed by demons.
A receptacle for torments,
A wet nerve
In the fires of suffering,
A mouth for screams.
You are silent
But you are mine. No need
That you stand here at the altar—
As bullocks wait
For the priest's knife.
Our prayers
Carry you like a fish in a net
To your fate.

The will of the Furies
Is fixed, like the sun.

As the sun's heat, as the sun's darkness
All feel it, in every twist
Of their fate.

There is no justice—
But ours. The pure man
Goes free, he does not interest us.
Only the sinner
Hiding his bloody hands,
Covering his head with his bloody hands,
We convict him. We drag
Out of his body the price
Of the blood he has shed.

Night is our mother.
We live in her womb.
We swoop out of her womb
To punish the living
Who walk about in daylight.
Apollo
Thinks he can steal our prey,
Our allotted victim.
But the one who killed
His own mother
Must answer to us.

Fate, who shapes everything
That happens on earth,
Appointed us
To do this work—
To rise out of the wound
In the murdered mother
And fasten our talons
In the eyeballs
Of that fool
Who struck blindly.
We ride him
Into the land of death—

And there we ride
His ghost for ever.

The immortal high gods
Have nothing to do with us.
They do not feast
At our feasts.
Among the white robes and the lustral brilliance
Of the temple rites
We are not to be found.
Made of darkness, clothed in darkness,
We rove along the flight paths
Of torment,
We follow war home,
And where the killing weapon refuses to rest,
Where it persists with its madness
Within a family,
Blood shedding its own blood,
We arrive,
Bringing the judgement of earth.

Our labours
Relieve the gods of a task that is pitiless.
Zeus abhors us
Though we do his work.
For Zeus, we howl
On the murderer's trail —
Or fall on that man, without warning,
Like the collapse of a house.
Out of the bodies of guilt
We crush justice.
We are guilt itself —
Blood of the blood
That has sinned.

A man in his splendour
Is like the sun.
But when the blood from someone he has killed

Spills into his conscience
He sinks into the black clouds of our tatters.
Then the living blood that beats in the head
Is the drum of vengeance.
His own hand, darkened by blood,
Covers his eyes.
His brain whirls in darkness.
Voices of the dead
Deepen his voice as he groans.

Law is everlasting
And we are the everlasting
Enforcers of the law.
We are hated.
But the law cannot bend or renounce its course.
The other gods keep to the bright air.
They steer clear of the dark
And rocky track down which we drive the living and the
    dead.

We have declared who we are
And what our duties are,
Obedient to fate.
We are to be feared and revered
And though we sleep
In the blindest cavern of earth
In the blink of an eye we are with you.

(Enter Athene.)

ATHENE

Who summoned me
With such a powerful voice?
This voice came to me beside the river Scamander
Where the chieftains
Had given me land, for my help in sacking Troy.
I came here in a moment,
Overtaking the swift winds.

And now I am astonished
By what I see. Who are you?
You, who cling to my effigy
Like a child clinging to his mother.

And you—creatures that cannot be described,
Like nothing that belongs on this earth
Or among the gods. But let me be just.
Let me remember the fair tongue of reason.

CHORUS
Daughter of Zeus, hear us.
We are the daughters of primeval darkness.
Our land is deep in the earth.
Men call us their curse.

ATHENE
I know you and I know what men say of you.

CHORUS
Perhaps you do. Now you shall hear our duties.

ATHENE
Be simple and clear.

CHORUS
We hunt all who commit murder.

ATHENE
Can your prey escape you?

CHORUS
Only where happiness was never known.

ATHENE
You are driving this man beyond that limit.

CHORUS
Orestes killed his mother deliberately.

ATHENE
Did no greater power force him to do it?

CHORUS
What power can madden a man to kill his mother?

ATHENE
Is this the case you present? Who speaks against you?

CHORUS
Try him. Hear the facts. Then give judgement.

ATHENE
But will you accept my decision?

CHORUS
We trust your Father's name and his great wisdom.

ATHENE
Orestes, speak.
You believe in my justice.
That is what brings you so far
To kneel here, like a statue fixed
At the foot of my statue.
Tell me first, your country,
Your breeding, your history.
Then reply to this charge.
And let your words be simple and clear.

ORESTES
Athene, Goddess of Divine Wisdom,
My hands are not fouled with blood.
I do not crouch here
Polluted with a crime.
The law forbids a homicide to speak
Till a ritual priest has showered him
With the blood of a suckling animal.
Over and over again, in other shrines,

I have kneeled under that shower.
Let it be known, then: I am ritually clean.

I was born in Argos.
You know my father—you joined with him
To crush Troy: Agamemnon.
Commander of the great fleet.
When he came home
And stripped to wash off the long war's weariness
My mother opened her arms
And enfolded him in a net—
Then killed him where he rolled, helpless, in the water.

I returned after years of exile.
I knew what had happened. I loved my father.
And Apollo had let me know
What I would suffer if I failed
To avenge his murder.
So I killed my mother.
Was I right or wrong?
Athene, be my judge.
I will accept your decision
Even though you pronounce my death.

ATHENE

This case is too deep for a man.
Nor should I let the law, like an axe,
Fall mechanically on a murderer.
Especially since you came to my temple
As a supplicant
Fully cleansed of your crime.
But your accusers have to be heard.
And if their case fails—what happens to their anger?
It whirls up into the air, it blackens heaven,
It falls like a plague on Athens.
Falls as a curse on Athens.
How am I to deal with the dilemma?
Let me select a jury of the wisest

Among the citizens of this city.
Let them be the first of a permanent court
Passing judgement on murder.
They shall be sworn in
To integrity and truth.
They shall have the full use of my wisdom.

(She goes.)

CHORUS

This is an evil day.
On this day
True and false
Exchange faces.
If this new jury, by some juggling,
Exculpate this killer,
His example will become a model—
A licence for homicides.
Children washing their hands
In the blood of their parents
Will thank Orestes
For opening this gate in the law
Through which they can walk blameless.

The Furies will sleep.
The guilty man will yawn, content.
Murder shall be relieved
Of its conscience—
While the citizens cower in their houses,
Afraid to walk the streets,
Or even to look out of the window
At a darkening future.

When the criminal rules, with absolute power,
It will be too late
To call for us.
Parents will utter their death-cries
To deaf ears.

While the jury debates right and wrong
And while soft-headed fools
Jabber about remedial measures
This new malefactor, licensed here,
Will charge the parents he murdered.
And he will win his case and prove them guilty.

Man cannot do good
Without fear of the consequences
Of doing evil.
If the work of man's hand
Is not supervised by the Furies
That hand will stop at nothing.
The man without fear of the law
Will easily kill, as if by nature.
And the city without fear of the law
Is that killer's playground.

Lawless freedom is evil.
The tyrant's penal code is evil.
Freedom in one pan of the balance,
Stern rule in the other—
Where these hang in equilibrium
The scales are in the hand of God.
An evil heart
Has an evil hand.
A good heart has a hand
Blessed and able to bless.

Before all other powers—
Worship Justice.
Never desecrate the divinity
Of Justice
By twisting it, for profit.
Everything is cause and effect.
Crime creates misery.
Let man cherish his father and his mother.

Let him honour the guest, and protect him.
Whoever loves the good
Will live in wealth and be respected.
Natural virtue
Has nothing to fear.
But the man who sets his own course
Across the laws
In defiance of Justice—
He will be wrecked.

He will be tossed in the ocean,
Voice lost in tempest,
Head lost in maelstrom—
God will smile
To see all the big words and noisy folly
Go off in bubbles
As the huge seas of affliction
Swallow him up.
Only his name, unmourned,
Will survive for a while
As a question, a caution.

(Enter Athene with twelve citizens.)

ATHENE

Herald—assemble the city:
Let one blast of your trumpet open heaven
And shake all Athens to its feet.

All jurors and citizens, you people of Athens,
Assemble in silence. Acknowledge what I have created
To serve men,
To establish justice now, and throughout all time to
    come.

(Enter Apollo.)

CHORUS

Apollo, look after your own affairs.
You have no right to a voice in this case.
Your presence here today is interference.

APOLLO

Let what I have to say decide that.
According to the law, this man, Orestes,
Is under my sacred protection.
Since I appointed the stroke of the sword-blade
That dispatched his mother, and since I
Cleansed him of the crime
And of all blame,
It is for me to argue his case.
Athene, open the proceedings.
And supervise them according to your wisdom.

ATHENE *(to Furies)*

You, the plaintiff, speak first.
The charge must be heard in full, and in all detail
By the whole court.

CHORUS

Many as we are, our words will be few and to the point.
You are bound to reply clearly to each question.
And our first question is this:
Did you or did you not kill your mother?

ORESTES

I cannot deny it. I killed her.

CHORUS

So there's the first round and we have won it.

ORESTES

Don't be too pleased with yourselves too quickly,
There is more to come.

CHORUS

Even so: describe to us how you killed her.

ORESTES

I stabbed her through the heart with my sword.

CHORUS

And who talked you into this act?

ORESTES

Apollo. He is my witness.
His oracle commanded me to do it.

CHORUS

The great god of prophecy and poetry
Persuaded you to matricide. Yes?

ORESTES

He did, and has protected me ever since.

CHORUS

You will think differently when this court condemns
    you.

ORESTES

He will not fail me. And my dead father helped me.

CHORUS

You acted for the dead? And killed your mother.

ORESTES

Her guilt was double, which doubled her sentence.

CHORUS

What do you mean? Explain yourself to the court.

ORESTES

She killed her husband. And she killed my father.

CHORUS

Her death paid for all. But you are alive.

ORESTES

While she lived, after she killed her husband
And my father—where were you and your justice?

CHORUS

We stir only for killers of their own blood kin.

ORESTES

Is my blood my mother's?

CHORUS

Butcher! You were made in her womb, by her blood.
How can you deny the blood your mother
Fed into your veins.

ORESTES

Apollo, tell them.
Prove that my act,
My killing her,
Was an act of justice.
Yes, I stabbed her.
But what words
Can justify me?
Make this clear,
Apollo, teach me
How to defend
What I have done.

APOLLO

Great court of Athene—
Let me speak as the god of prophecy.
All my words are just and true. My oracle
Never declared to any man or woman,
Or to any city, one word
God had not first approved.
So it was with what I said to Orestes.

Remember too,
No oath or other earthly consideration
Can counter the nod of Zeus.

Are you saying that Zeus
Dictated the words that you dictated
Through your oracle?
Are you saying
That Clytemnestra, remembering Iphigenia,
Had no case, when she murdered Agamemnon?
That Justice could not hear her
Till Orestes had avenged Agamemnon?

The rods of Zeus are law.
The two deaths—
Of Agamemnon and of Clytemnestra—
Are utterly different from each other.
He was a King, invested in divine right.
To be killed by a woman
Might have been honourable, but only in battle.
He was killed otherwise.
Athene, you who are judging this matter,
Hear now how it happened.
Agamemnon had returned, triumphant,
From the long war.
He had cleansed his battle-stained body
In the ritual bath.
Clytemnestra attended him, in this cleansing.
But then, as he stepped out of the bath,
One foot out of the water, at that moment
She flung a robe of mesh around his body,
Wound and bound him in a tangle of folds
And pushed him backwards. Helpless he fell into the
     bath.
And there, as he wallowed, netted in the water,
She drove her sword through him. Three times.

Citizens, and you who sit on the jury,
You twelve who are here to judge Orestes,
This was how the father of Orestes died,
Whose royal eye had launched the vast fleet
And steered a whole army across oceans.
And now you know what kind of woman killed him.

CHORUS

You are saying: Zeus values only the father.
Yet how did Zeus treat his own father?
When Cronos became old
Zeus bound him not with a net of silk
But with a net of chains—
Bound him and castrated him.
When did fathers become so precious?
Jurors, do you hear?

APOLLO

Filthy witches—rubbish of creation.
Chains can be unwound
But blood cannot be recalled
From the dust.
Once the life is out, you cannot relight it.
Death is the only ailment
For which Zeus appointed no cure.

CHORUS

What has this to do with it?
Only think—
How will a matricide
Live in his father's house, in Argos?
Will he join the religious rites?
Will he wash his hands at the feasts with lustral water?

APOLLO

Listen patiently.
The son is said to belong to his mother—
But she is not the real parent.

She is the nurse.
She is like the soil in the pot
Where the seed germinates, and the plant springs,
The seed planted there by the father.
If the child lives, the mother
Continues to tend it, and nurse it—
As the plant is kept in the pot till it flowers.
The mother is incidental.
She may be entirely unnecessary—
As with Athene
Who sprang from the head of Zeus
Without a helping touch from any woman's hand.
Athene, I sent this man to plead at your altar.
I shall send many other gifts
To make the fame of Athens resound.
Befriend him and you have befriended all Argos.
His posterity will not forget it.

ATHENE

The moment has come for the jurors
To consult their conscience, and cast their vote.
Have plaintiff and defendant finished?

APOLLO

I shall abide by the jurors' verdict.

ATHENE

Are you happy to hear the jurors
Make their judgement?

CHORUS

The jury has heard. As they cast their vote
Let them remember their oath. And let them
Also remember the primal laws of the earth.

ATHENE

Citizens of Athens!
This is the first case of homicide

To be tried in the court I have established.
This court is yours.
From today every homicide
Shall be tried before this jury
Of twelve Athenians.
And this is where you shall sit, on the hill of Ares.
When the Amazons came as an army
To be avenged on Theseus
This is where they set up their camp
And built an altar to Ares.
And therefore this rocky height is named
Areopagus.
Here my laws shall stand
Unchanged through the hours of the days, the days of
    the years.
And awe, that humbles the heart,
With fear, the brother of awe, from this day
Shall keep the pride of Athenians in check.
Where a pure spring is polluted
By a filthy trickle
No man will drink, or can drink without being
    poisoned.
I open on this rock
The pure spring of my laws.
Do not taint them
By any expedient shift for advantages.
Protect this court
Which will protect you all
From the headstrong licence of any man's will
And from slavery.
Above all, remember the power of fear
And cherish it in your ministry of the laws.
The man who need not fear the consequences
Of anything he does
Brings his evil dreams into the open,
He lets them play in the sun,
But finally he sets them to work
Among men, among his family,

Among his own tribe. It is fear
That crowns the law with a halo of sanctity.
In this court you have a fortress
Possessed by no other people—
From the cold Northern fringes of Phrygia
To the outermost twinkling rocks of the Peloponnese.
I give you this court and I bless it—
Like heaven, not to be violated.
Like heaven, holy,
And like heaven vigilant, quick to anger and to punish,
A sleepless, armed, unconquerable guard
Over the peace of men and their families.

I have spoken at length
So Athens will remember my words.
Now set your hearts in your oath
And give judgement. Cast your vote
Without your whole being in heaven.
I have spoken.

(They vote.)

CHORUS

I warn you
We are visitors to your land, we are your guests.
Fear our anger. Fear it.
Fear the law of our anger.

APOLLO

And you—do not forget
Your fear of Zeus, who prompted me
To speak through my oracle to Orestes.
Remember your fear of God.

CHORUS

Bloody murders have nothing to do with you.
Orestes is polluted. Orestes
Polluted your shrine. Your shrine is polluted.

APOLLO

You are forgetting
How Zeus purified
The first of all murderers—Ixion.
Was Zeus polluted?

CHORUS

You are the god of winged words—
Fletched and barbed words.
But if we lose this judgement
This land, and the city of Athens,
Will decay. We shall blast it—with a curse.
Such a curse, life itself
Will be agony, the very nerves of life
Will be instruments of torture.

APOLLO

The old gods detest you
As much as we, the younger gods, detest you.
We shall win this judgement.

CHORUS

With a bribe, it may be,
As once before, in the house of Admetos,
You bribed the Fates
To restore to life a dead woman.

APOLLO

Admetos worshipped me—I was justified.
There was no crime, and Admetos' need was great.

CHORUS

You are young, we are old.
You think you can trample us down.
When I have heard the verdict
That will be the moment soon enough,
To avenge myself on Athens.

ATHENE

I have the final casting vote.
You jurors, after your votes are counted,
My vote goes for Orestes.
I am unknown to any mother.
In my reckoning,
The death of a woman who killed her husband
Weighs nothing
Against the death of her victim.
The father's right, prerogative of the male,
Has my vote.
If the votes of the jury are equal
My vote gives the judgement to Orestes.
Bring the urns and count the votes.

ORESTES

O Apollo, what will the verdict be?

CHORUS

O Mother Night, O Darkness, we are your voice.

ORESTES

Out of all my life, within this minute
My life or death is decided. Hope or despair.

CHORUS

For us—our renown is renewed
Or our powers are annulled
And our fury scattered through the earth.

APOLLO

The vote is cast.
Citizens, count with care.
Your sorting is sacrosanct—
Where justice is divine.
Loss of a single vote
Will bring a man's life down in ruins.

One vote gained will raise the ruins of a life
To a future of good fortune.

(The vote is counted.)

ATHENE

The jury is divided equally—
Between the accused and the plaintiff.
Therefore my vote decides it.
Orestes is acquitted.

ORESTES

Athene—
You are the new foundation of Agamemnon's
Resurrected house.
You have given an exile his own home.
Now it can be said:
Orestes is an Argive. Orestes
Upholds his father's throne
Blessed by Athene and Apollo together,
And by the All-Father, Zeus.
Great Zeus has redeemed my dead father
From my mother's crime.
God himself has exonerated me
Of all guilt.
I am going back to Argos
But before I go let me swear this:
For all time to come, Attica
Shall be the beloved friend of Argos.
No Argive shall ever carry a weapon
Against Attica. Whoever breaks this oath
With which I bind all the posterity of Argos
Shall be ruined by my curse.
My ghost shall come back from the dead
To break his spirit on the march, his body in the battle.
But all Argives who honour this oath
Shall live in my blessing.
And for you, people of Athens, I pray:

May all your enemies be humbled. For you
May the word 'battle' and the word 'victory'
Be for ever one.

(Apollo and Orestes go.)

CHORUS

The earth is overthrown.
Our laws are obsolete.
You younger gods
Who argue us out of court,
And rob us of what is ours—
You violate creation!
You dishonour the voice
Of the blood and the earth.
Now that voice
Shall burst through this land like a mass madness,
It shall fall, as if from heaven,
In a deadly rain
On plant and beast and child.
Earth's whole face shall be one canker.

I shall not weep for Athens
Where this forum
Of slippery orations
Mocking justice
Was invented.
I shall not weep
For the folly of Athens
When the daughters of darkness,
The voices of blood and the earth,
Take their revenge.

ATHENE

Noble ladies, I beseech you,
Suspend your anger till you have heard me speak.
This even vote, fairly arrived at,
Is no humiliation to you.

How could Orestes not be saved
When the great god who ordered him to strike
Reveals the hand of Zeus
Signing the warrant?
Let your rage pass into understanding
As into the coloured clouds of a sunset,
Promising a fair tomorrow.
Do not let it fall
As a rain of sterility and anguish
On Attica.
Accept this verdict
And here in Athens, the envied city,
You shall have a permanent home.
You shall sit on thrones of dignity
In a sacred cavern, and receive
Tributes of gratitude and honour
For ever, from all our people.

CHORUS

Our old laws are crushed under the new.
Our justice is buried, like the ashes of Troy.
The voice of the blood, that you have banished,
Cries from the stones.
But that buried voice
Shall rise like a miasma
And fall on this land as a madness
And as a contagion.
I shall not weep
When the scream of all living creatures
Goes up from Attica.

ATHENE

You have not been crushed or insulted.
Your voice has not been buried.
There is no reason
Your deathless fury
Should punish this land.

You call for justice.
But God speaks through me.
Only I, Pallas Athene,
Possess the key
That unlocks the thunderbolt of Zeus.
But the time of brute force
Is past.
The day of reasoned persuasion,
With its long vision,
With its mercy, its forgiveness,
Has arrived.
The word hurled in anger shall be caught
In a net of gentle words,
Words of quiet strength.
The angry mouth shall be given a full hearing.
I understand your fury.
But the vendetta cannot end,
The bloody weapon cannot be set aside
Till all understand it.
You will thank me for this
When the harvest of Attica
Lays its first fruits on your altar,
When marriage and childbirth—
The two sacraments
By which societies perpetuate
Their people and their bonds to each other—
Make their sacrifices at your shrine.

CHORUS

Apollo's priestess sniffs up the fumes
That open her to the god.
But we breathe the exhalations
Of the living blood.
They are our life, as blood is the life of man.
Can we be shut away inside the earth,
Voiceless and nameless
Under a temple paved with words,

Under columns of reasonable persuasion?
Earth sees our humiliation.
Our anger shall shatter the floor of the temple
Of the new gods
And we shall not weep
When the great scream of everything that lives
Is screamed in Attica.

ATHENE

I bow
To your great age, so much greater than my own.
I bow
To your wisdom, which is nourished
By the first stirrings in the earth's womb,
And is so much greater than mine.
Though God gave me, too, some small insight.
But if you leave Athens
You will know your mistake.
The greatness and glory of Athens
Is a dawn glow in the East—
The first light of its approaching, amazing day
Touches the wall of this temple.
If you live here
In a sanctuary, prepared for you,
You shall be cherished
As nowhere else on earth.
You shall be acknowledged,
You shall be honoured
At marriage and childbirth—
Those oldest sacraments of blood,
Where strangers are united in love
And a new being is brought out of chaos.
All shall pay you tribute.

Do not madden our young men
With the hiss of the whetstone
And the dream of the plunging blade.
Do not swell their pride

With the dream of purging themselves
Of all their bodily violence
In the rapture of battle.
Do not addict them
To the drug of danger—
The dream of the enemy
That has to be crushed, like a herb,
Before they can smell freedom.
Do not inflame them
With the foolish temper of the fighting cock
That sets faction against faction
Within the one city of families—
All for nothing—
The numbed and pitiless carnage
Of civil war.
Great Goddesses of the blood
Your home is here, in Athens, the city
Which all the gods love best.
And here you shall be counted among the gods,
Among the greatest, among the most honoured.

CHORUS

We cannot live on words.
Nothing can nourish us
Except the exhalations
Of the dead and the living blood.
Nothing can alter the blood.

ATHENE

Listen to my words, which shall never be other than
　　gentle.
You are the oldest gods.
You shall not complain
That younger gods banished you,
Discredited and homeless, from this land.
Listen to persuasion, the sacred balm
That heals self-wounding anger.
Be patient with eloquence,

Drink its sweetness, and be quieted.
Live here with us.
If you reject my words
You have no argument to justify
Your taking revenge on Athens.
Athens offers you all that gods could hope for,
Your reputation glorified in this city,
And Justice itself made greater here
Because it is hospitable to your truth.

CHORUS
Athene, what is this cavern?

ATHENE
A place to be loved. It is yours if you want it.

CHORUS
What rights come with it, if we accept it?

ATHENE
No family shall flourish without your favour.

CHORUS
This place, and this power — are these your promise?

ATHENE
All who honour you — I will honour.

CHORUS
Can this promise be kept?

ATHENE
Athene
Promises nothing she cannot perform.

CHORUS
Your words have stirred us. They have melted our anger.

ATHENE
Here in Athens you are among friends.

CHORUS
Let us bless Attica. How shall we bless this land?

ATHENE
Send Victory—without remorse.
Let the earth bless Attica.
Let the heavens and the seas bless it.
The wind and the sunlight, let them bless it.
Let crop and beast bless it
With abundance.
Let it be blessed with young warriors
To guard its peace.
Root out the godless, the lawless—
Do not let their overgrowth choke out
The flower of the good.
Let the lives of all just citizens
Flow from beginning to end undistorted
By lies or twisty dealing.
Ensure these blessings,
Then leave it to me to make the name of Athens
Resound throughout the world, and throughout all time.

CHORUS
Let us live in Athens and bless Athens,
The home of Athene.
With Zeus and Ares
And all the gods of Greece
Through the centuries to come.
Let Athene's name, and the name of Athens,
Resound throughout the nations.

ATHENE
I welcome to Athens
These terrible powers, the implacable,

The unappeasable
Goddesses, the powers of darkness
Who have risen from the earth
To watch over the ways of mankind.
The man who angers them
Lives in misery,
His days a curse—
Ignorant why
The whiplash cuts
Across his heart.
The hidden guilt of his father
Splays him on their altar
To be judged.
And for all his cries of innocence
His life is taken as the payment.

CHORUS

We can give more.
We can preserve
Your orchards,
Your forests.
We can bring health to your flocks and herds.
We can persuade great Pan
To bring twin lambs
From every ewe.

ATHENE

Athens—hear the blessings that are the gift
Of these dreadful creatures.
Fate's executioners are swayed
By neither heaven nor hell.
They deal with mankind
Here on earth
And mankind weeps to acknowledge
That they give to men and women
What they have earned, neither more nor less:
Songs to some,
Screams to others.

My prayers move the earth
To cherish and protect
The living seed of man
And the womb of woman.
My prayers move
The three daughters of Earth
Whose fingers touch into place
The destiny of everything born.

ATHENE

I rejoice to hear
Your changed voices.
Your terrifying voices
Becoming kindly.
And I bless
The sacred power of persuasion
That makes calm the storm in the body.
The presence of God in persuasion
Draws the poison fangs of evil,
Undoes the knotted mesh of brooding hatred.
In the gentle combat of persuasion
Good wins over good with goodness
And none lose.

CHORUS

Never let civil war, the most
Malignant of all misunderstandings,
Divide Athens.
There is no hope nor future
For a land
Whose mind is split
Into two, and where each half
Strives only to destroy the other.
Give Athens a single mind, a whole mind,
As a marriage
Gives to two strangers
One child.

ATHENE

These appalling creatures
Are wise.
Dreadful as they are
They bring a huge wealth
To Athens. Worship them and thank them.
They will return
Kindness for kindness.
Only let Athens
Be founded in justice
And everything in Attica shall flourish.

CHORUS

Athens—beloved of Athene—
Sits between the feet
Of Zeus, the God of Justice,
Like his best-loved child.

ATHENE

Come to your home in the rock,
Torch-lit. You noble women
Enter the cavern.
Live with us, powerful to repel
From Attica
All misfortune.
Citizens of Athens,
Welcome the kindly ones.
They will bless our land and city.
Bless them. Bless them.

CHORUS

And we bless all
Who live in this city,
Who love this rock,
Who walk with the gods.
All who fear us
And welcome us, all

Whose prayers are humble,
We shall bless you.

We thank you.
Now by torches we lead you to your home under the
    earth.
Young women, the most beautiful,
And children, the joyful,
Form our procession, brighter than the torches.
And older women, robed in purple,
Go with us.
Honour the friendly ones.
Let the blazing procession go in.
Lead our guests to their new home
Where they shall administer
Great wealth, great good fortune
To Attica.

Daughters of timeless darkness,
Enter your subterranean home.
You who know what honour is
And why honour is holy,
Enter the fortress of understanding.
Into the earth,
The cavern timeless as the tomb
Where sacrifices shall be offered up
In religious awe
That makes the words of dedication holy.

Terrible kindly ones,
Come to your rest
In the flame of torches
And let the voice of every citizen,
With a shout of welcome, be made holy.

Pour out the wine.
Let the pine bough crack and blaze.

Zeus, Father of All,
Guards the city of Athens.
So God and Fate, in a divine marriage,
Are made one in the flesh
Of all our people—
And the voice of their shout is single and holy.

Made in the USA
Las Vegas, NV
19 January 2023

65905219R00122